MW01503305

Special Kids' Stuff

high-interest, low-vocabulary, reading & language skills activities

by cherrie Farnette, Imogene forte
And Barbara Loss

INCENTIVE PUBLICATIONS, Inc.

P.O. Box 12522
NASHVILLE, TENNESSEE 37212

ACKNOWLEDGMENTS

Special acknowledgment is gratefully accorded to:

Bobbie Grubb, typist, critic and friend, whose contribution
to this effort has been boundless.

Bill Washington, whose artistic flair is reflected in many
of the illustrations in the book.

Joy MacKenzie, for the cover design and concept, and for
her never-failing creative support.

Library of Congress Catalog Number 76-505
        ISBN Number 0-913916-20-X

Copyright© 1976 by Incentive Publications. All rights reserved.
Printed in Nashville, Tennessee, United States of America. No part
of this publication may be reproduced, stored in a retrieval system, or
transmitted, in any form or by any means, electronic, mechanical,
photocopying, recording, or otherwise, without prior written permission
of Incentive Publications except as noted below.

Pages bearing these symbols (NOW   WOW   POW)
were designed by the authors to be used as PUPIL ACTIVITY PAGES.
It is intended that copies be made of these pages for individuals or groups
of pupils. Permission is hereby granted--with the purchase of one copy
of SPECIAL KIDS' STUFF, HIGH INTEREST-LOW VOCABULARY READING
AND LANGUAGE SKILLS ACTIVITIES--to reproduce copies of any pages
bearing these symbols in sufficient quantity for classroom use.

Printed in Nashville, Tennessee
United States of America

PREFACE

Special Stuff is a special kind of book written for special students.
It is a collection of learning experiences designed to help boys and girls
use basic communication skills in a relaxed and meaningful manner. A
simple format featuring easy-to-follow directions and limited vocabulary
is utilized to introduce contemporary topics of high interest to the students.
Each of the learning experiences is presented at three or more levels of
difficulty to provide for differing student readiness stages. Student
activity pages are designated by the following symbols:

These symbols have been used to denote levels of difficulty in presentation
of content and skill development. is the basic knowledge level
with intellectual and creative expectancies ascending in this order, ,
and then   The coding system will enable teachers to quickly
select and adapt experiences to meet widely varying readiness stages.
Students needing additional practice in a particular skill area may work
through the entire set of activities without stigma while other students move
on to related enrichment activities.

Teachers and students will enjoy working together to devise study projects,
contracts or learning center objectives unique to individual student needs
and interests. In some instances it may be desirable to allow students
complete freedom to work through as many of the activities in a given set
as time permits and/or interest is maintained. Other situations may call
for a diagnostic-prescriptive approach. For example, in heterogeneous
classroom settings the activities may be presented to existing instructional
groups and/or to especially created interest groups. Academically talented
students will appreciate the humor and opportunity for creative development
of many of the center activities. Homogeneously grouped students with
learning disabilities may well profit from more teacher direction in
selection and completion of activities in keeping with their abilities. In
cases of severely handicapped students, teachers may find it appropriate
to select activities to be presented in a one-to-one tutorial setting. Teachers
concerned with mainstreaming students with limited abilities or experiences
into the regular classroom will find the high interest-low vocabulary
activities extremely valuable.

The activity cards, readiness experiences, and puzzles found in the Appendix
offer additional simple but challenging reinforcing experiences. They are
especially designed to encourage students with differing ability levels to
work together in a harmonious and creative manner resulting in a mutual
sense of success.

By now you have probably discovered that the authors of Special Stuff really believe that ALL KIDS ARE SPECIAL. This book is an outgrowth of that belief and of our desire to contribute in some small measure to the joy of learning for special kids and special teachers we know and would like to know.

Cherrie Farnette
Imogene Forte
Barbara Loss

Nashville, Tennessee
March, 1976

Extra Stuff → Many of the activities include additional suggestions for skills reinforcement and are designed to be used as student options.

TABLE OF CONTENTS

III.   WORD RECOGNITION AND USAGE

Classification Turn About

CENTRAL PURPOSE:

Classification

CENTER OBJECTIVES:

After completing this center the student should be able to:

(1) classify words and phrases.
(2) classify ideas.
(3) develop categories.
(4) make functional use of words in a given category.

PROCEDURE:

1. Place activity sheets, pencils, and dictionaries in the center.

2. Verbally introduce the center and devote as much time as necessary to developing the understanding of classroom skills.

3. Provide time for evaluation of each completed activity.

4. Ask the student to select a friend to share the completed activity sheets with before they are filed.

Write the names of the pictures in the correct puzzle boxes.

Words to use:

coat	shirt	glove	blouse	belt
dress	hat	skirt	sweater	jacket
pants	socks	shoe	apron	

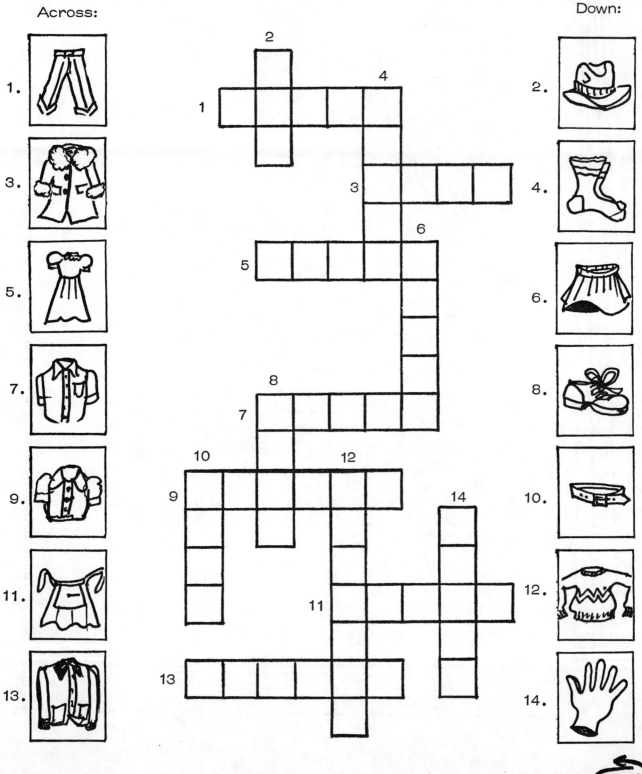

Across:

Down:

NOW

The words in each triangle have something in common. They all belong to the same category. Name the words to a friend and ask him to guess the category.

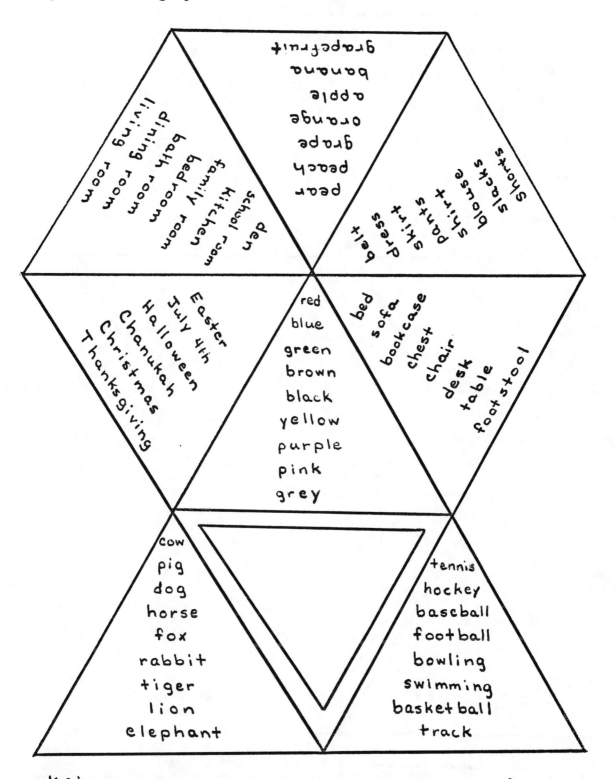

Instead of telling your partner the words listed in each category, give clues and ask him to guess the words. After he has guessed the words ask him what they have in common.

WOW

Cut out the category triangles. Select a triangle and name the items belonging to that category.

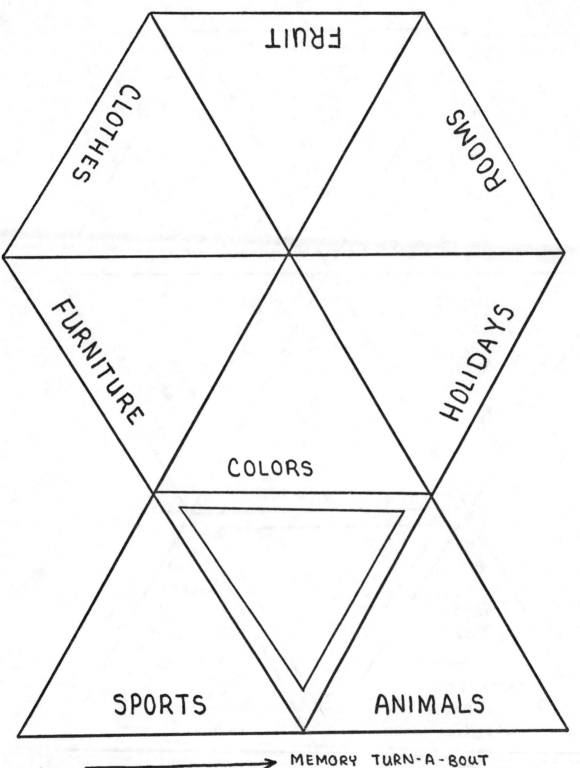

FRUIT

CLOTHES

ROOMS

FURNITURE

HOLIDAYS

COLORS

SPORTS

ANIMALS

MEMORY TURN-A-BOUT

Extra Stuff To make this a game, choose a partner and take turns naming items in the category. The winner is the person who names the most items without repetition.

WOW

14

Select a triangle and fill it with words that belong in that category.

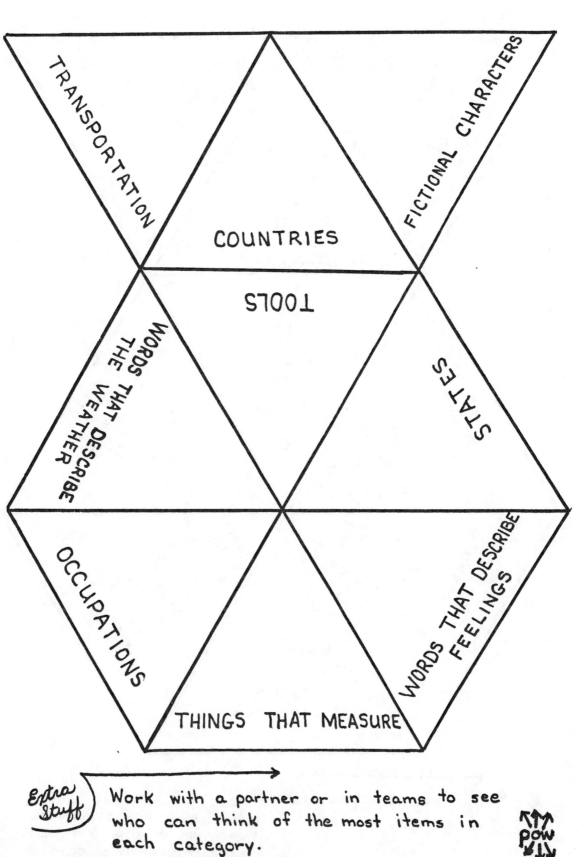

Extra Stuff → Work with a partner or in teams to see who can think of the most items in each category.

POW

Choose a triangle and read the words to a friend. Ask him to tell what the words have in common and to name their category.

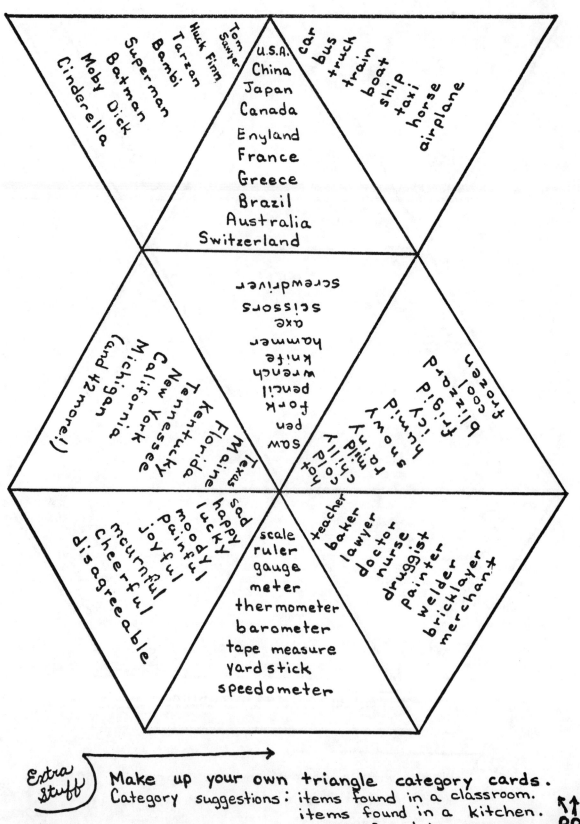

Extra Stuff) Make up your own triangle category cards.
Category suggestions: items found in a classroom.
items found in a kitchen.
items found in a car.

16

POW

Context Connections

CENTRAL PURPOSE:

Using Context Clues

CENTER OBJECTIVES:

After completing this center the student should be able to:

(1)   use pictures as context clues.
(2)   complete sentences by using context clues.
(3)   use context clues to select appropriate words to complete sentences.

PROCEDURE:

1.   Place activity sheets, reference books, and pencils in the center.

2.   Verbally introduce the center and explain each of the center activities.

3.   Arrange time for evaluation of each completed activity and give immediate feedback.

4.   Make provision for sharing and filing completed activities.

Circle the picture that completes each sentence.

A mailman delivers

A bird lays

She drank

A boy read a

He rode in a

Pilots fly in a

Circle the picture that completes each sentence. Write in the missing words.

I answered the ringing _____.

To get some fresh air he opened the _____.

Before he read the letter he opened the _____.

To carry water from the well he used a _____.

It was raining so I took my _____.

Astronauts fly to the _____.

The hungry squirrel ran up the _____.

The carpenter hit the nail with a _____.

19

Find words in the "word mixer" to complete each sentence.

1. Joe _____ his _____ to town.

2. Jan _____ with _____ dolls.

3. Tony _____ bread and _____ milk.

4. The _____ jumped on the _____ ledge.

5. Jim hit the _____ _____ his bat.

6. Cindy ran _____ the playground _____ swing.

7. The _____ and stars shine at _____ .

8. Mr. Smith _____ to pick up his _____ that the wind

   had blown _____ the street.

Extra Stuff) Write five other sentences using words in the word mixer.

20

Double Talk

CENTRAL PURPOSE:

Mental Imagery

CENTER OBJECTIVES:

After completing the center the student should be able to:

(1)   relate to figurative language.
(2)   associate figurative language and pictures.
(3)   make decisions related to the use of language references.

PROCEDURE:

1.   Place activity sheets, pencils, crayons, and construction paper in the center.

2.   Verbally introduce the center.

3.   Plan time for discussion and evaluation of each completed activity and provide additional reinforcement as needed.

4.   Assist the student in making a decorative construction paper cover for the completed activity sheets. This makes a "fun" activity package to share with family or friends.

Draw a line from each descriptive phrase to the picture that illustrates it.

hungry as a bear

busy as a beaver

working like a dog

free as the wind

fresh as a daisy

happy as a lark

sweet as sugar

pretty as a picture

fit as a fiddle

clear as glass

NOW

Some words can be used in "funny ways". Write the phrase that best describes each picture.

Phrases to use:

"beside himself"
"beat the drum"   "starry eyed"   "in the doghouse"
"two faced"   "mad money"   "for crying out loud"
                   "brainstorm"

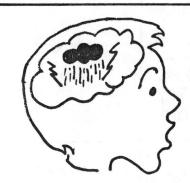

Read each set of sentences.
Circle the word that is the same.
Draw a line from each sentence to the picture that describes it.

	If you're not careful, you'll slip! Sue wore a slip under her dress.	
	Quick, stamp out that bug! Sam put a stamp on the letter.	
	The task was to match the shapes. We need a match for starting a fire.	
	The dress shop was having a big sale. She went to shop for groceries.	
	You must pick up everything you drop! Each drop told of her sadness.	
	Tim took time to watch his favorite show. Willy got a new watch.	
	Pam bought a pound of coffee. Pound the hammer to get attention!	
	Tom and Tim went outside to play ball. We enjoyed watching the play.	

24

Hear Ye! Hear Ye!

CENTRAL PURPOSE:

Critical Listening

CENTER OBJECTIVES:

After completing this center the student should be able to:

(1) listen to find answers to questions.
(2) gain specific information from oral reading.
(3) make inferences and draw conclusions.

PROCEDURE:

1. Place activity sheets and pencils in the center.

2. To provide motivation and develop readiness for the center, read aloud a selection from a familiar book and ask the students to answer questions related to the story.

3. Explain the center carefully to enable two students to work together to complete the activities.

4. Encourage students to use basal readers, library books, or social studies texts to select stories or chapters to be used in a similar manner.

Read this story to a friend.
Ask him to answer the questions at the end of the story.

Joe and Sam made plans to play ball together. When Joe went to meet Sam, his friend was not there. He went to Sam's house and rang the doorbell.

Sam's mother came to the door and said, "Hello, Joe. Sam has a bad cold and can't go outside. He must stay in bed."

Joe was disappointed. He would have to wait to play ball with his friend on another day.

Questions:

1. Were Joe and Sam friends? _____

2. Did Sam's mother have a cold? _____

3. Was Joe able to come out and play? _____

4. Was Joe happy? _____

5. Who's who? Find a picture of Joe. Find a picture of Sam.

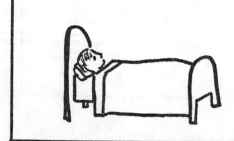 

NOW

Read the list of questions to a friend.

Ask him to listen as you read the story aloud to try to find answers to the questions.

> One day Tom was happily listening to his portable radio. His little brother came over and grabbed the radio away.
>
> Tom yelled angrily, "No, that's mine. I had it first. Give me that radio back."
>
> He pushed his brother down. The radio fell on the floor and broke into many little pieces.
>
> Now both brothers were angry and sad.

Questions:

1. What was Tom listening to?

2. What did his little brother do?

3. What happened to the radio?

4. Why were the boys angry?

5. Why were the boys sad?

6. Number the pictures in the order that best describes how Tom felt during the story.

Extra Stuff Role play this story with a friend. Show how you feel through your actions - happy, sad, angry, or surprised.

27

WOW

Read this story to a friend.

Ask him to answer the questions at the end of the story.

It was Bob's birthday and he couldn't wait to find out what special present his parents had bought for him.

"What is my present?" Bob asked his mother over and over again.

"It's a surprise," she said. "I'll give you a hint, though. Your present has wheels and you can ride it."

Bob thought and thought. What could the surprise be? It had wheels. You can ride it. Maybe it was a big shiny car like his dad's.

"No," thought Bob, "I am too little to drive a car."

Maybe it was a fast, noisy motorcycle like his big brother's. But Bob was too little to drive a motorcycle.

Maybe it was a boat to take on the lake. No. It couldn't be. Boats don't have wheels.

He thought and thought. What has wheels and is just right for a boy his size to ride. He couldn't guess what the birthday present was. Can you?

Questions:

1. Why was the day special for Bob?

2. The surprise present wasn't a car like Dad's. Why?

3. Why couldn't Bob's present be a motorcycle?

4. It couldn't be a boat. Why?

5. What do you think the present was? Why?

6. Find a picture of the surprise present.

Non-Sensational

CENTRAL PURPOSE:

Making Value Judgments

CENTER OBJECTIVES:

After completing this center the student should be able to:

(1)   relate sentences to pictures.
(2)   distinguish between sense and nonsense.
(3)   change nonsense sentences to sentences that make sense.

PROCEDURE:

1.   Place activity sheets, pencils, art paper, and pastel tempera paints in the center.

2.   Introduce the center to enable the student to complete activities as independently as possible.

3.   Provide time for ongoing guidance and evaluation.

4.   Ask the student to use the art paper and tempera paints to devise an attractive folder to hold completed activity sheets.

Read these nonsense sentences.

Circle the word in each sentence that is not correct.

1. Don't full down the stairs.

2. The waiter put the foot on the table.

3. All that food makes me fall.

4. I picked up a pan and started to write.

5. I mist you.

6. Tank you.

7. Little grills are made of sugar and spice.

8. Of horse, you can do it.

9. I poured water in my cap.

10. The cupboard was bear.

11. I gave my hog a bone.

12. I live you.

13. Sting a song.

 Rewrite the sentences so that they make sense.

Shoe Shopping With Sandy

Sandy wants a special shoe. She can't remember the name of the shoe she wants. All she knows is what she doesn't want!

Read these statements and put an X on each shoe that she does <u>not</u> want.

Sandy says:

"I don't want a boot."

"I don't want a sandal."

"I don't want a ballet shoe."

"I don't want a shoe with words."

"I don't want an ice skate."

"I don't want a lady's high heel."

"I don't want a moccasin."

"I don't want a shoe with a buckle."

"I don't want a shoe with dots."

"I don't want a football shoe."

Circle the shoe that is left to find out what Sandy wants to buy.

 What will Sandy do with her special shoe?

_____

Read these sentences to a friend. See if he can tell you what is wrong. Ask him to correct each statement so that it makes sense.

1. I am bigger than a house and smaller than a bread box.

2. I drank the sandwich and ate the milk.

3. The weather report predicted showers so I went to the store to buy some soap.

4. Smell me a story.

5. I got out of the car and drove away.

6. I turned off the switch and the light went on.

7. I put my sandwich in the refrigerator and sat down to eat it.

8. I put on my gloves to keep my feet warm.

9. I had such a nice train ride across the ocean.

10. I called you on the telephone so that I could see you.

11. I wanted to get a higher salary so I took my ladder to work.

12. I was hungry so I went to the library.

13. It was such a hot day that I turned on the heat.

14. Listen to the picture and look at the sound.

Extra Stuff → Choose a "foolish thought" and illustrate it with a drawing of your own.

WOW →

Read these nonsense sentences.

Rewrite the sentences so that they make sense.

NONSENSE SENTENCE	SENSIBLE SENTENCE
1. Don't cry over spelled milk.	1.
2. I was tired sew I took a map.	2.
3. You deserve a brake today.	3.
4. If you're stick go to bad.	4.
5. I tore the ham in my coat.	5.
6. I licked an ice scream comb.	6.
7. Pardon me, but your ship is showing.	7.
8. We need some light. Please burn on the lamb.	8.
9. If the shoe fats, where it.	9.
10. You made your bread, now lye in it.	10.
11. Mother went into the kitchen to fly the chicken.	11.
12. I lake to sale on the like.	12.

Extra Stuff → Make up your own nonsense sentences.

Willy often says the opposite of what he means to say.
Read the story to see how "wrong" words get him into
trouble.

In the morning Willy went to school and said,

"Good <u>night</u>, Mrs. Jones. Here is an apple for

you because you are such a nice <u>man.</u> I like you

because you are a very <u>bad</u> teacher--and <u>ugly</u> too!"

When the bell rang, Mrs. Jones took the roll. When

she called Willy's name, he raised his hand and

said, "I'm <u>absent</u> today."

After lunch Mrs. Jones said, "Willy, you failed the

test again. You always give the opposite answer."

Willy lowered his head and sadly said, "I feel <u>happy</u>

about that. You're <u>wrong.</u> I'll study <u>less</u> next time."

Rewrite the story using these words in place of the underlined words:

present	unhappy	more	morning
right	pretty	good	lady

34

Read this story to a friend.
Ask him to stop you each time there is something wrong in the story.
See if he can change the wording so that the story makes sense.

SILLY FARMER JONES

Farmer Jones put on his rain boots because it was such a sunny, dry day. He went to the barn to feed his children. The chickens said "quack" as he milked the family horse. The farmer then went into the playground to feed the pigs and to see if the cow had laid some eggs for his breakfast.

Farmer Jones went back to his house and his wife fixed him scrambled bacon and tossed eggs. He finished drinking his paper and read the coffee.

After his meal, Farmer Jones got into his bed and drove to town. He went to the barber shop to have his grass cut and to talk to his friend, the chair.

At sunrise the farmer went to sleep because he had put in a full day's work and he was so wide awake.

Extra Stuff

Select your favorite sentence in this crazy story and illustrate it.

35

Make up your own nonsense sentences.

Ask a friend to rewrite the sentences so they make sense.

1.	1.
2.	2.
3.	3.
4.	4.
5.	5.
6.	6.
7.	7.
	8.
9.	9.
10.	10.
11.	11.
12.	12.

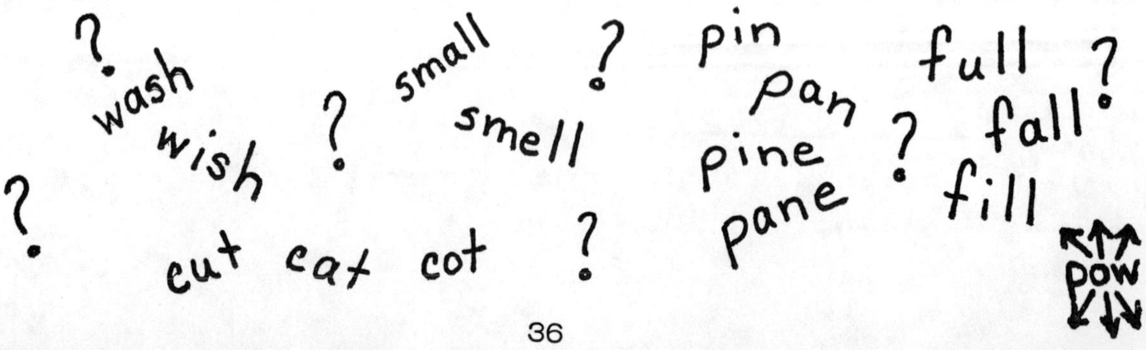

? wash wish ? small ? smell ? pin pan full ? pine ? fall ? pane fill

? cut eat cot ?

POW

36

Next Step

CENTRAL PURPOSE:

Sequencing

CENTER OBJECTIVES:

After completing the center the student should be able to:

(1) use picture clues to develop and tell a story with plot and sequence.
(2) order and reorder picture clues to develop and tell a story in more than one way.
(3) make a creative contribution to sequenced picture clues to be used in the development of an original story.

PROCEDURE:

1. Place activity sheets, pencils, crayons, magazines, paste, scissors, and extra paper in the center.

2. Verbally introduce the center.

3. Arrange conference time for discussion and evaluation of each completed activity and provide additional reinforcement as needed.

4. Make provision for sharing picture sequences in a group setting and for filing or displaying all completed activity sheets.

Start with the boy sitting on the ball.
Follow the maze.
Tell a story to go with the pictures.

START

NOW

38

1. Use these pictures to tell a story.
2. Number the pictures in the order the story is told.
3. Reorder the pictures so that the one you had first is last and tell the story in another way.

What happens next?

WOW

1. Tell what happened in each picture sequence.
2. Tell what might happen next in each sequence.
3. Draw pictures to illustrate what you have described.

What happens next?

Extra Stuff — Use cartoons and magazine pictures to make a sequence story.

POW

Pict-O-Gram

CENTRAL PURPOSE:

Picture-Word Associations

CENTER OBJECTIVES:

After completing this center the student should be able to:

(1)   match words and pictures.
(2)   associate symbols with words.
(3)   use word and symbol associations to read a story.
(4)   use picture symbols to create an original story.

PROCEDURE:

1.   Place activity sheets and pencils in the center.

2.   Discuss the pictures and symbols in as much detail as necessary to enable the student to complete the activities.

3.   Arrange for two students to work together to complete the activities and to "check" each other's completed work.

4.   Make provision for filing or displaying completed activity sheets.

Picture and Symbol List

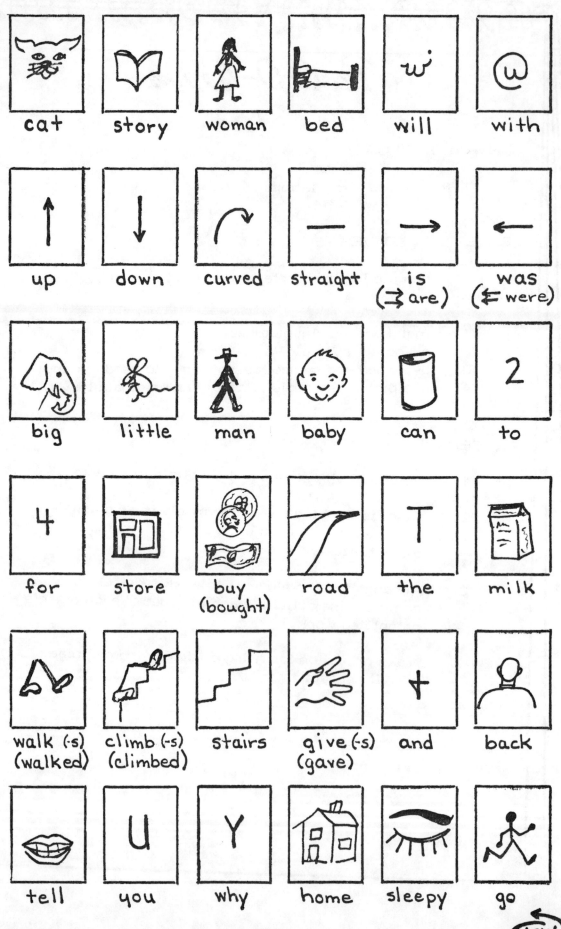

cat	story	woman	bed	will	with
up	down	curved	straight	is (⇉ are)	was (⇇ were)
big	little	man	baby	can	to
for	store	buy (bought)	road	the	milk
walk (-s) (walked)	climb (-s) (climbed)	stairs	give (-s) (gave)	and	back
tell	you	why	home	sleepy	go

NOW

Use the Picture and Symbol List to match the words with the correct pictures.

can
big
little
buy
climb
tell
give
back
walk
home
store
go
sleepy
man
woman
stairs
road
story

NOW

Use the Picture and Symbol List to match each word with the correct symbol.

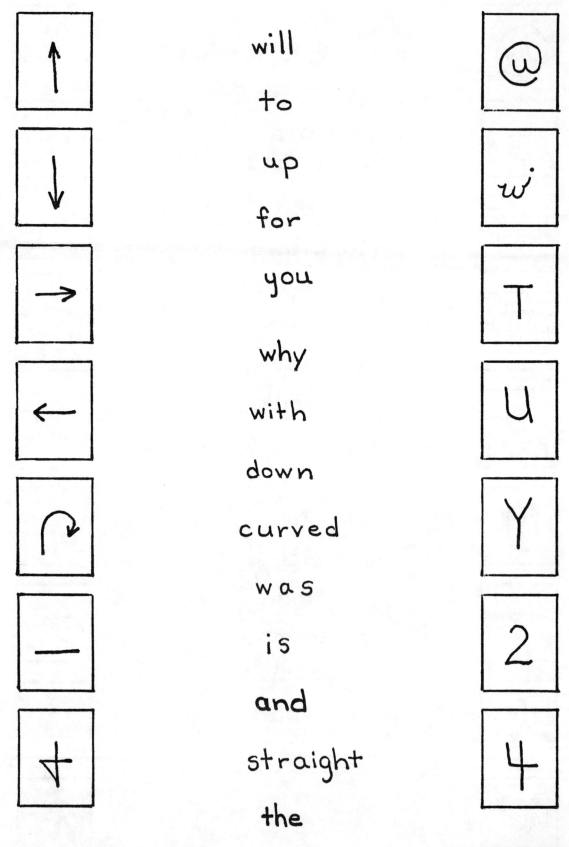

will

to

up

for

you

why

with

down

curved

was

is

and

straight

the

WOW

Use the Picture and Symbol List to read this story. Write the correct word under each picture.

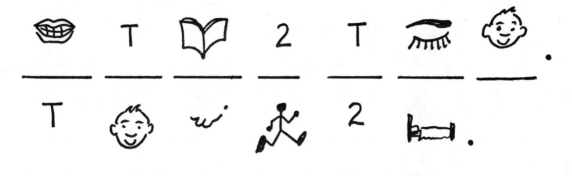

_____ _____ _____ _____ _____ _____ _____ .

_____ _____ _____ _____ _____ _____ .

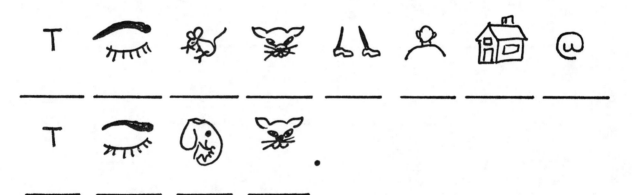

_____ _____ _____ _____ _____ _____ _____ _____

_____ _____ _____ _____ .

_____ _____ _____ _____ _____ _____ _____ _____

_____ . _____ _____ _____ _____ _____ _____

_____ _____ .

_____ _____

45

Here is another story for you to read.

Make your own picture and symbol list. Try to make your list as creative as possible.

47

Write your own pict-o-story. Use pictures and symbols from your own picture and symbol list.

Ask a friend to read your story.

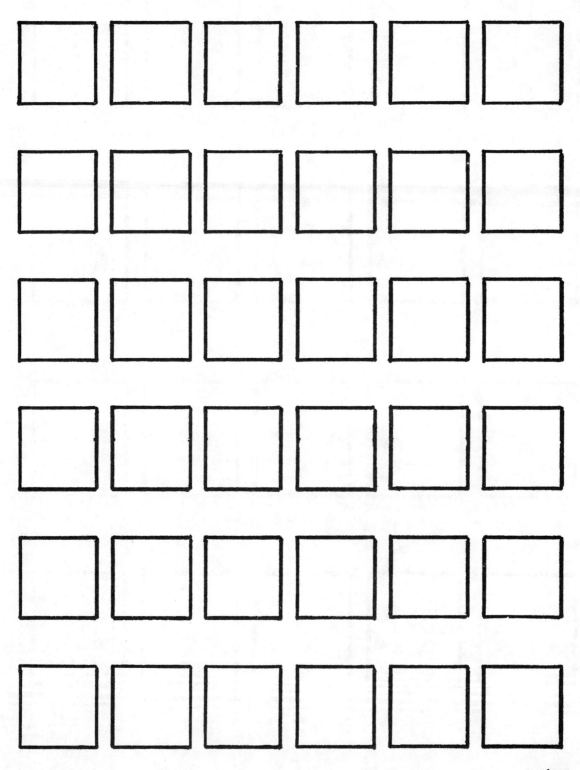

Question Box

CENTRAL PURPOSE:

Critical Reading

CENTER OBJECTIVES:

After completing this center the student should be able to:

(1)   use visual clues to find answers to questions.
(2)   use context clues to find answers to questions.
(3)   note details in order to gain information.
(4)   find answers to questions by drawing inferences from written material.

PROCEDURE:

1.   Place activity sheet, pencils, extra paper, and a loose leaf notebook entitled "Question Box Stories" in the center.

2.   Verbally introduce the center and discuss sample items to enable the student to complete the activities as independently as possible.

3.   Arrange for ongoing guidance and evaluation.

4.   Make provision for filing or displaying completed activity sheets. Add creative stories to the "Question Box Stories" collection.

Read the story to find answers to these questions.

What happened at 9:00 in the morning? _____

_____

What happened at 9:00 at night? _____

_____

Where did the boy put his toys? _____

How many hours did he work? _____

Extra Stuff) Write a story about what will happen next. ⟶

NOW

Why did the cat leave home? _____

_____

List three reasons why he came back home.

1. _____

2. _____

3. _____

TITLE: _____

Answer these questions:

1. Why did Hattie want to wear a hat to school?

2. Why did her mother want her to take an umbrella?

3. How did the other students feel about her hat?

4. What happened on the way home from school?

5. Describe how Hattie felt after she got home?

6. Give the story a title.

WANT TO PLAY?

Give five reasons why Joey had no friends.

_____   _____

_____   _____

_____

If you were Joey, what would you do to make friends? _____

_____

Write another title for this story. _____

The first men to have success in flying an airplane were Wilbur and Orville Wright. This first flight was at Kitty Hawk, North Carolina on December 17, 1903. Charles Lindberg was the first aviator to cross the Atlantic Ocean. This flight was on May 21, 1927.

The first operational jet airplanes were introduced by the German Air Force in 1945. DeHavilland Comet Airliners, flying for a British Airline, introduced the jet age to civilians in the 1950s.

On July 20, 1969 Neil Armstrong was flung into orbit around the moon by a large rocket. He landed on the moon with the aid of small rockets and left his footprint on another world.

American and Russian astronauts demonstrated the growth from flight in air to flight in space by orbiting the earth together in July of 1975.

List the six important flight events given in the report above. Give their dates.

1. _____

2. _____

3. _____

4. _____

5. _____

6. _____

Extra Stuff) Use your dictionary to look up any unfamiliar words found in this report.

Reader's Choice

CENTER PURPOSE:

Analogies

CENTER OBJECTIVES:

After completing this center the student should be able to:

(1)   associate related concepts.
(2)   infer relationships in order to complete thoughts.
(3)   draw conclusions.

PROCEDURE:

1.   Place activity sheets, pencils, poster paper, and colored chalk in the center.

2.   Verbally introduce the center.

3.   Instruct the student to select a partner to work with and to follow the activity directions.

4.   Arrange time for discussion and ongoing evaluation of activities and provide individual guidance and reinforcement as needed.

5.   Make provision for sharing ideas in a group setting and for filing completed activity sheets.

Circle the picture that completes each analogy.

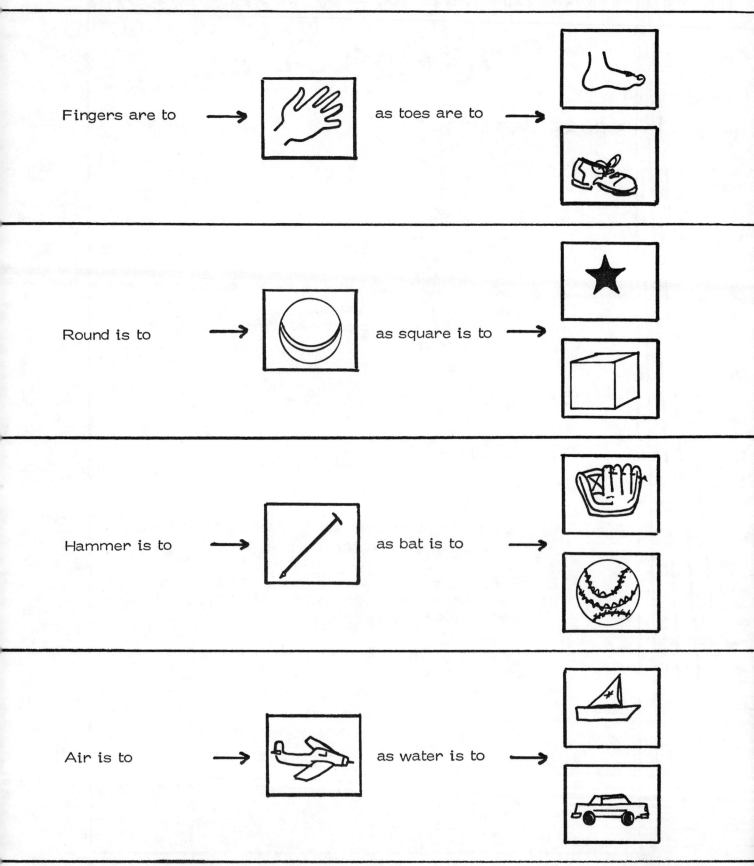

Fingers are to →   as toes are to →

Round is to →   as square is to →

Hammer is to →   as bat is to →

Air is to →   as water is to →

Circle the correct word to complete each analogy.

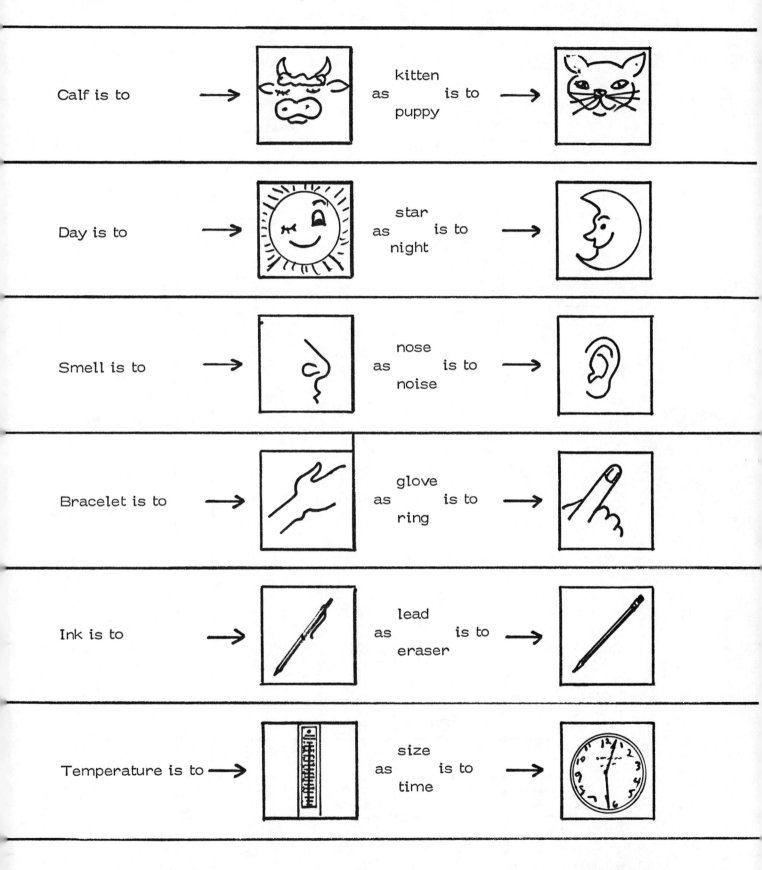

Calf is to → [cow] as kitten / puppy is to → [cat]

Day is to → [sun] as star / night is to → [moon]

Smell is to → [nose] as nose / noise is to → [ear]

Bracelet is to → [wrist] as glove / ring is to → [finger]

Ink is to → [pen] as lead / eraser is to → [pencil]

Temperature is to → [thermometer] as size / time is to → [clock]

Find the color words to complete these phrases, and write the correct words in the puzzle boxes.

Across

1. _____ as grass
3. _____ as dirt
5. _____ is for girls
7. _____ grape juice
9. _____ hot

Down

2. sunshine _____
4. _____ skies
6. _____ as snow
8. _____ as night
10. _____ as a pumpkin

Color Words

red
blue
orange
black
white
green
brown
pink
yellow
purple

Extra Stuff Think of other items which these color words might describe.

58

Fill in the missing word to make each statement true.

Words to use:

fall	south	hear
go	ear	window
happy		dark

Talking is to the mouth

as

Hearing is to the _____.

Red is to stop

as

Green is to _____.

East is to west

as

North is to _____.

A frown is to sad

as

A smile is to _____.

A rug is to a floor

as

A curtain is to a _____.

White is to black

as

Light is to _____.

A book is to read

as

A record is to _____.

Summer is to winter

as

Spring is to _____.

Fill in the missing word to make each statement true.

A dictionary is to words

as

An _____ is to maps.

Low is to a valley

as

High is to a _____ .

Tracks are to a train

as

_____ are to a car.

Electricity is to a television

as

_____ is to a car.

North America is to Canada

as

_____ is to Brazil.

Washington, D. C. is to the
United States of America

as

_____ is to Mexico.

Leaving is to departing

as

_____ is to arriving.

Boy is to "son"

as

_____ is to "daughter".

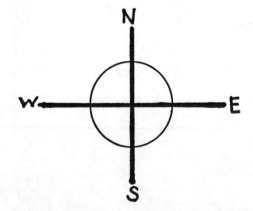

Riddle Roundup

CENTRAL PURPOSE:

Drawing Inferences

CENTER OBJECTIVES:

After completing this center the student should be able to:

(1)   read to reach conclusions.
(2)   set purposes to guide listening and thinking.
(3)   use context clues to make independent judgments.

PROCEDURE:

1.   Place activity sheets, pencils, dictionary, and two or three riddle books in the center.

2.   Lead a discussion of riddles and share the riddle books as motivation for the center activities. Discuss the center in detail and ask the student to work with a friend to complete the activities. Encourage student independence by suggesting the use of the dictionary if help is needed to correctly spell answers to the riddles.

3.   Make provision for filing or displaying completed activity sheets.

4.   Ask the student to develop additional "Riddle Roundup" work sheets to be placed in the center, to find a riddle book in the library to add to the center collection, or to select a favorite riddle to illustrate.

Read the clues to a friend.
Ask him to guess who you are.

I wear a badge.
I wear a uniform.
I direct traffic.
Safety is my job.
My car has a siren and a
    flashing light.

I am a _ _ _ _ _ _ _ _.

My color is red.
I slide down poles.
I ride in a truck.
I work with water, a hose,
    and ladders.
I put out fires.

I am a _ _ _ _ _ _ _.

Which hat would I wear?

What is not a tool of my trade?

I wear white.
I carry a black bag.
Health is my business.
I work in a hospital:
A nurse is my helper.

I am a _ _ _ _ _ _.

I work in an office.
I work with brushes.
I work with drills.
When you come to see me, you
    open your mouth.
Teeth are my business.

I am a _ _ _ _ _ _ _.

What is a tool of my trade?

Which part of your body do I help?

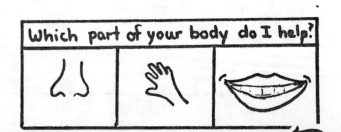

NOW

Read the clues to a friend.
Ask him to tell what season you are describing.

Birds fly north.
Days are longer and warmer.
The wind blows and kites fly.
Showers bring flowers.

Colors change from grey to
    green.
The ground hog looks for his
    shadow as a sign of

    _ _ _ _ _ _ .

Days are short and nights are long.
Warm clothes must be worn.
Rain turns to ice and snow.
I am best known for my color
    of white.

Snowmen, sleds, and a new year
    are signs of

    _ _ _ _ _ _ .

Days are long and the
    temperature rises.
It is a time for outdoor play.

Swimming is a favorite sport.
Heavy clothes are not for me!
Picnics, camping and carefree
    days are signs of

    _ _ _ _ _ _ .

Days grow shorter and sweaters
    are worn.
Leaves change color and start to
    fall.
When I begin, so does school.

Animals prepare for winter.
Ghosts, goblins, turkeys and
    feasts are signs of

    _ _ _ _ _ _ .

Extra Stuff Name the pictured holidays and the season in which they belong.

Solve these riddles.

Word Clues:

wheel	corner	clock	telephone
chair	window	flag	floor
tree	mirror	pencil	

What Am I?

1. I have legs and a back, but cannot walk.

2. People see through my panes.

3. You may know me by my bark, but I make no sound.

4. People walk all over me, but I don't mind.

5. I can fly, but I need a pole.

6. I have a ring, but no fingers.

7. I tell time, but cannot speak.

8. The sharper I get the shorter I become.

9. I look like you until you go away.

10. I travel many places, but always go in circles.

11. I am always in a place where two things meet, but no one ever says "hello".

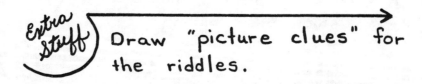

Extra stuff) Draw "picture clues" for the riddles.

64

State Your Position

CENTRAL PURPOSE:

Using Position Words

CENTER OBJECTIVES:

After completing this center the student should be able to:

(1)   use position words in a problem-solving setting.
(2)   follow directions featuring position words.
(3)   use position words to express original thoughts.

PROCEDURE:

1.   Place activity sheets, pencils and red felt tip markers in the center.

2.   Verbally introduce the center and play a game using position words to develop readiness for the center activities.

3.   Arrange for two students to work together to complete the activities and to check each other's work.

4.   Make provision for filing or displaying completed activities.

Follow these directions to find your way through the maze.

1. Find the boy sitting beside the water.
2. Find the girl who is going into the water.
3. Next go to the girl who is in the water.
4. Move to the girl who is in the water and running after the ball.
5. Find the girl who is on top of the water.
6. Draw a red circle around the other person who is out of the water.

Extra Stuff — Ask your friend to retell the story by describing what each person is doing.

NOW

Cut out the hat and the "newspaper".
Cut along the dotted lines to make four slots.
Give a copy of this activity to a friend and ask him to follow these directions
as you read them to him.

1. Put the hat on the man's head.
2. Put the newspaper over his stomach.
3. Put the hat on top of the newspaper.
4. Now, put the hat beside the newspaper.
5. Put the hat under the newspaper.

As your friend follows each direction, ask him to use position words such
as "on", "over", "under", and "beside" to tell where the man, the hat,
and the newspaper are in relation to the other items.

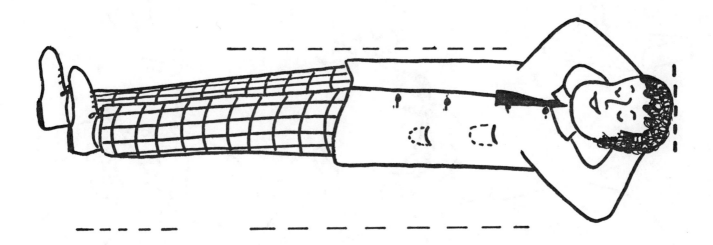

DAILY NEWS

Weather   Big News

fold in middle

Today's Paper Says   more News

WOW

Give a copy of this activity sheet to a friend.
Ask him to find each picture as you tell him about it.
Be sure to use position words to help make your descriptions
easier   to follow.

Detail Discovery

CENTRAL PURPOSE:

Detail Awareness

CENTER OBJECTIVES:

After completing the center activities the student should be able to:

(1)   verbally note likenesses and differences.
(2)   discover and list common physical likenesses.
(3)   use descriptive detail in personal communication.
(4)   use listening skills to gather information.

PROCEDURE:

1.   Place activity sheets, pencils, art supplies, records, and phonograph in the center.

2.   Verbally introduce the center.

3.   Arrange time for discussion and ongoing evaluation of each activity and provide reinforcement as needed.

4.   Encourage the student to use art supplies of his choice to add interest to the completed activities before they are shared or filed in keeping with the center provision.

Ask a friend to complete this activity with you. Discuss how the two pictures in each box are the same and how they are different.

NOW

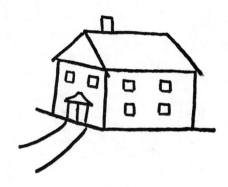

Choose a house and describe it to a friend. See if he can find the exact house that you are talking about.

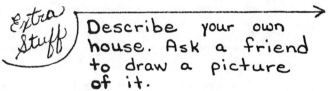

Extra Stuff Describe your own house. Ask a friend to draw a picture of it.

NOW

Listen to your favorite song. Write the words being sung (lyrics) in the record below.

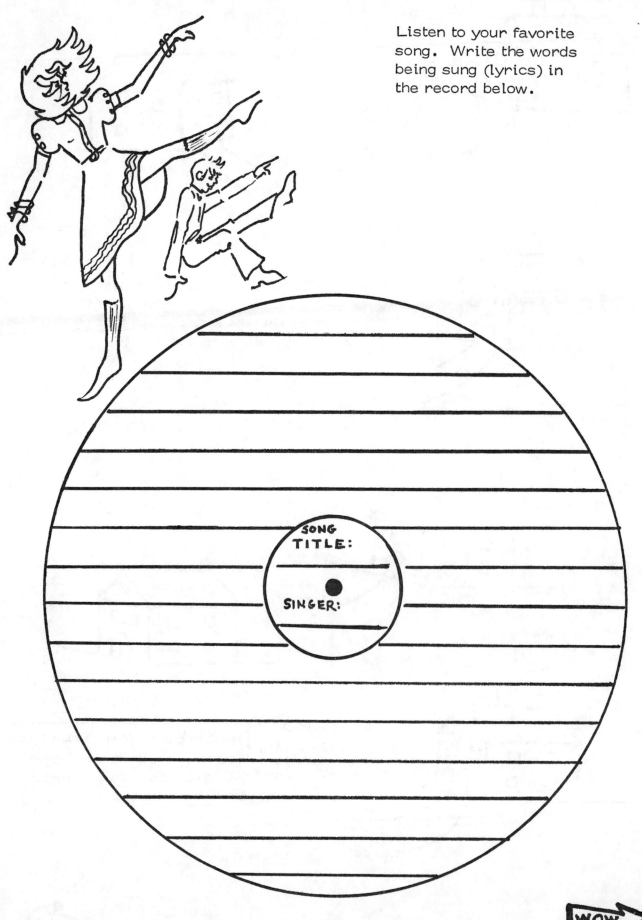

SONG TITLE:

SINGER:

WOW

74

Match the twins.
List three things each set of twins has in common.

WOW

Listen to radio or television broadcasts.
"Picture" the programs in words or drawings
by completing this questionnaire.

Review a program of your choice.

1. Name of program _____
2. Type of program _____
3. TV or radio station _____
4. Time and date of program _____
5. Summary of story _____

Sports Item

1. Game reviewed _____
2. Who played? _____
3. What was the final score? _____
4. What were the outstanding plays? _____

News Item

1. Issue (What happened?) _____
2. Who was involved? _____
3. Where did it happen? _____
4. When did it happen? _____
5. Why did it happen? _____
6. How will it affect you? _____

Weather Report

1. Forecast for today _____
2. What is the high and low temperature of the day? _____
3. What was the weather yesterday? _____
4. What is the prediction for tomorrow? _____

Commercial

1. What is the product being sold? _____
2. Why are we supposed to buy the product? _____
3. To what group of people does the commercial appeal? _____
4. What did you like about the commercial? _____
5. What did you not like about the commercial? _____

Home Sweet Home

CENTRAL PURPOSE:

Idea Association

CENTER OBJECTIVES:

After completing the center activities the student should
be able to:

(1)   associate ideas and pictures.
(2)   extend ideas into complete thoughts.
(3)   develop and refine associations to form a creative
        concept.

PROCEDURE:

1.   Prepare a large bulletin board near the center
       with the heading "Home Sweet Home".

2.   Place activity sheets, pencils, dictionaries, and
       art supplies in the center.

3.   Verbally introduce the center.

4.   Arrange time for discussion and ongoing evaluation
       of each activity.

5.   Make provision for sharing completed activity
       sheets in a small group setting.

6.   Ask the student to add a creative story to the bulletin
       board display. The completed display should
       stimulate lively classroom discussion and could
       well be used as the focus for creative dramatics,
       a mural, or a poetry collection.

Describe each "home" by telling who lives there, what it is made of, and where it is likely to be located.

Who:

What:

Where:

Who:

What:

Where:

Who:

What:

Where:

Who:

What:

Where:

Who:

What:

Where:

Who:

What:

Where:

Look in the windows and write a
sentence describing the people
who live in each apartment.

79

Write a paragraph about what you might find if you visited someone living in this house.

_____

_____

_____

_____

_____

_____

_____

_____

_____

_____

_____

Imagi-Station

CENTRAL PURPOSE:

Creative Thinking

CENTER OBJECTIVES:

After completing the center activities the student should be able to:

(1)   express original thoughts.
(2)   organize creative thinking within a topical framework.
(3)   develop a creative story with plot and sequence.
(4)   express personal awareness of differing points of view.

PROCEDURE:

1.   Place activity sheets, pencils, crayons, dictionaries, and a large scrapbook in the center.

2.   Lead a group discussion of the center and its objectives to encourage creative use. Extend the discussion to focus on separate activities and provide guidance as needed.

3.   Make provision for evaluating and sharing completed activities in a group setting and encourage the student to select a favorite to include in the Imagi-Station scrapbook.

Before

After

Name:

Age:

Weight:

Name:

Age:

Weight:

This girl went to a "super" beauty shop. Fill in the information for each picture. Write a paragraph telling how the girl looked "before" and a paragraph telling how she looked "after" the "beauty" treatment.

Before

_____

_____

_____

_____

_____

After

_____

_____

_____

_____

_____

Write a story about what you would wish for if you were granted two wishes.

Look at the picture and use your imagination to finish the story.

PICKLE EATER

I won the pickle eating
contest, but _____

_____

_____

_____

_____

_____

_____

_____

_____

_____

_____

_____

_____

 Think of other contests that you could
win and write stories about them.

Look at the picture. Use your imagination to write a story to go with the last sentence that has been written for you. Give your story a title.

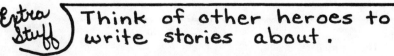

I saved the cat, but I got stuck in the tree!

Extra Stuff) Think of other heroes to write stories about.

Use this picture, one of these ideas, and your imagination to write a story.

- The score was twelve to twelve. There were only five minutes left in the game...
- I picked up the ball and started to run...
- I was enjoying the game when all of a sudden...
- Boy, was I embarrassed when...
- She knew nothing about football...

_____

_____

_____

_____

_____

_____

_____

_____

_____

_____

_____

Write two stories describing two different points of view of what is happening in the picture.

I was on the top of the human pyramid...

_____

_____

_____

_____

_____

_____

I was at the bottom of the human pyramid...

_____

_____

_____

_____

_____

_____

_____

POW

Write today's horoscope for each sign.

Aquarius, the water bearer	Leo, the lion
January 20- February 18	July 23- August 22
Pisces, the fishes	Virgo, the virgin
February 19- March 20	August 23- September 22
Aries, the ram	Libra, the balance
March 21- April 20	September 23- October 22
Taurus, the bull	Scorpio, the scorpion
April 21- May 20	October 23- November 21
Gemini, the twins	Sagittarius, the archer
May 21- June 21	November 22- December 21
Cancer, the crab	Capricorn, the goat
June 22- July 22	December 22- January 19

 Check your forecasts with those given in the newspaper.

Job Market

CENTRAL PURPOSE:

Career Awareness

CENTER OBJECTIVES:

After completing the center activities the student should be able to:

(1)   develop awareness of job demands.
(2)   express thoughts related to career "fitness".
(3)   complete a simple job application form.

PROCEDURE:

1.   Place activity sheets, pencils, high interest—low vocabulary books dealing with various careers, dictionaries, and art supplies in the center.

2.   Lead a group discussion focused on different types of occupations and occupational demands.

3.   Verbally introduce the center.

4.   Arrange time for discussion and ongoing evaluation of each activity and provide reinforcement as needed.

5.   Make provision for filing or sharing completed activities.

Draw a picture of yourself at work in a job you would like to have when you are twenty-one years old.

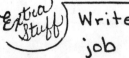 Write a paragraph describing the job responsiblities.

Read the application filled out by Joanne for a babysitting job. Think of a job you would like to have and fill out the application at the bottom of the page.

NAME: _Jones, Joanne Marie_ BIRTHDATE: _Jan. 11, 1965_
(Last,   First   Middle)

ADDRESS: _11 South Road_ PHONE: _222-3333_

JOB APPLIED FOR: _babysitting_

SALARY EXPECTED: _75¢ an hour_ STARTING DATE: _today_

EDUCATIONAL BACKGROUND:

kindergarten - Early School

grades 1-6 - Poke Elementary School

PAST EXPERIENCES:

Place	Job	Dates	Why did you leave?
Mrs. Smith's house	babysitting	June 3 & June 5	job over
Brown's house	dog sitting	August 7-13	their vacation over

REFERENCES:

Person	Address
Mrs. Jones (my mother)	11 South Road
Mrs. Brown	12 South Road

NAME: _____ BIRTHDATE: _____
(Last,   First   Middle)

ADDRESS: _____ PHONE: _____

JOB APPLIED FOR: _____

SALARY EXPECTED: _____ STARTING DATE: _____

EDUCATIONAL BACKGROUND:

PAST EXPERIENCES:

Place	Job	Dates	Why did you leave?

REFERENCES:

Person	Address

NOW

Mary is interviewing for a job.

List four reasons why you think she may not get the job.

1. _____

_____

2. _____

_____

3. _____

_____

4. _____

_____

Bill wants a summer job. He may have some problems.

Give him some suggestions for his next job interview.

_____

_____

_____

_____

_____

_____

_____

_____

Write a newspaper advertisement for the "Help Wanted" section of the newspaper for persons to fill the following positions:

WANTED: High School Football Coach; must be _____

_____

_____

_____

WANTED: Good Seamstress to work in ladies' specialty dress shop;

_____

_____

_____

WANTED: Experienced Chef for exclusive restaurant; _____

_____

_____

_____

WANTED: Math Tutor for sixth grade student; _____

_____

_____

_____

News Special

CENTRAL PURPOSE:

Newspaper Appreciation

CENTER OBJECTIVES:

After completing the center activities the student should
be able to:

(1)   develop understanding and appreciation of the
        newspaper and its influence on daily life.
(2)   read a newspaper to gain specific information.
(3)   organize facts and ideas to write news articles
        and feature stories.
(4)   express creative thoughts.

PROCEDURE:

1.   Place activity sheets, pencils, several newspapers,
       dictionaries, and art supplies in the center.

2.   Lead a group discussion of local, national, and
       special newspapers and their influence on personal
       thought and actions.

3.   Verbally introduce the center.

4.   Arrange conference time for evaluation of each
       completed activity and give reinforcement as needed.

5.   Make provision for sharing completed newspapers
       in a group setting and for discussion of ideas
       expressed and concepts gained.

6.   Ask the student to take the completed newspaper home
       to share with family or friends.

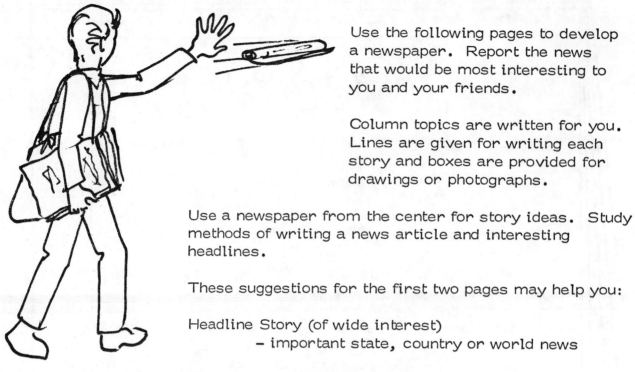

Use the following pages to develop a newspaper. Report the news that would be most interesting to you and your friends.

Column topics are written for you. Lines are given for writing each story and boxes are provided for drawings or photographs.

Use a newspaper from the center for story ideas. Study methods of writing a news article and interesting headlines.

These suggestions for the first two pages may help you:

Headline Story (of wide interest)
    – important state, country or world news

Local News (of local interest)
    – important school, neighborhood, or city news

Index
    – List the articles in NEWS SPECIAL in alphabetical order. Give the page number where each article can be found.

Editor's Column
    – A chance to give personal opinions. Take a written "stand" about: rules, parents and children, teachers and students, past or future events, issues of the day, and other debatable topics.

Of Special Interest – People in the News
    – Biographies of teachers; principals; friends
    – Birthdays
    – Reports on Community Helpers or political figures

Weather Report
    – Local weather information

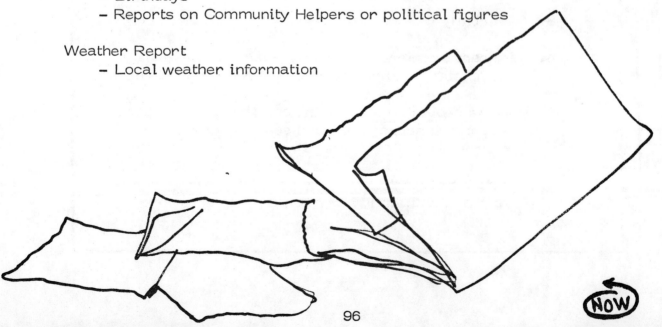

NEWS SPECIAL

City:
State:

Vol. _____ No. _____ Date _____

Headline: _____

Headline Story →
_____
_____
_____
_____
_____
_____
_____
_____

News Story Picture

Local News →
_____
_____
_____
_____
_____
_____
_____
_____
_____

Index

NOW

Comic Strip
Title ⟶   drawn by

Joke of the Day ☺

⟵ Special Puzzle ⟶

Sent in by _____

"Talk"
to
Tillie

Problem...

Answer...

Write to Tillie at this address:_____

NOW

3-NEWS SPECIAL

T.V. Guide ———————
→ Special Shows

Time	Program	Description
___ A.M.		
___ A.M.		
___ P.M.		
___ P.M.		
___ P.M.		

Favorite Program Review ——————→
→

_____
_____
_____
_____
_____
_____
_____
_____
_____
_____
_____
_____
_____

About the Stars ★ ★ ★ ★
Favorite Entertainer Review

★ ★ ★ ★ ★ ★ ★ ★ ★ ★

Movie Ads ——————→

WOW →

Sports Report

_____

_____

_____

_____

_____

_____

_____

_____

_____

What's In — Fashions and Fads

WOW

Local Talent →

Book Review →

Reviewed by _____

Title: _____

Author: _____

_____

_____

_____

_____

_____

_____

Favorite Records

_____

_____

_____

School Art →

WOW →

Editor's Column:
(expressing how we feel)

Of Special Interest
→ People in the News

Weather Report
The weather in brief:

Today: _____

Tomorrow: _____

Today's Temperature:
High _____

Low _____

pow

← Classified Advertisements →

Personal Messages

Jobs Available

Household Items for Sale

Houses for Sale

Used Cars for Sale

Pets for Sale

POW

Be a creative news reporter. Use your imagination. Add more pages
to your paper.

Pop~Ups

CENTRAL PURPOSE:

Vocabulary Development

CENTER OBJECTIVES:

After completing the center activities the student should be able to:

(1)   enjoy verbal word usage in both sense and nonsense settings.
(2)   select words to express complete thoughts.
(3)   complete a story with plot and sequence.

PROCEDURE:

1.   Place activity sheets, pencils, and art supplies in the center.

2.   Discuss the activity sheets and vocabulary in a group setting.

3.   Arrange for two students to work together to complete the activities and to "check" each other's completed work.

4.   Make provision for filing or displaying completed activities.

STORIES

POP-IT WORDS

BUZZ

BANG

HA HA

BOO HOO

MEOW

OUCH

RIVET RIVET

MOO

CLUCK CLUCK

Read these stories to a friend. Ask your friend to first choose pop-it words to make a silly story. Ask him to then choose the correct word to make a story that makes sense.

A bee flew by and went "_____". If a bee stings me, I'll yell, "_____".

When the baby was hot and tired he said "_____". His mother gave him a bottle and his funny toy and he said "_____".

A frog sat on a lily pad. "_____", he said. "I wish I were a cow and could say '_____', or a chicken and say '_____', or a cat and say '_____'."

The balloon went _____ when it burst into pieces. It scared the little girl so she cried "_____".

NOW

POP [ ] IN

Read these phrases to a friend.
Ask him to fill in the missing words.

(a) To make silly phrases, let him choose
any "pop-in" words.

(b) To make phrases that make sense, ask
him to choose the correct word for each
blank.

"NICE" THINGS TO SAY

1. "That's such a _____ hat, and you look
so _____ in it!"

2. "I had such a _____ time. Thank you for
being so _____ ."

3. "That was such a _____ movie. I can't
wait to tell my _____ friends."

4. "It's such a _____ day. Why don't we
take a _____ stroll."

5. "It was so _____ meeting you!"

Read this story with a friend and use the "pop-in"
words to fill in the blanks. Make a silly story and
one that makes sense.

THE _____ HOUSE

I felt _____ as I opened the _____
door of the _____ , _____ house.
The _____ wind was blowing the
_____ shutters and the moonlight cast
_____ shadows through the _____
windows.

I don't believe in _____ stories about
ghosts. But I know that I heard a _____ howl
and _____ footsteps on the stairs.

I ran out of that _____ door and back to my
own _____ house and hid under my
_____ bed.

POP - IN WORDS

- best
- haunted
- heavy
- squeaky
- scary
- broken
- chilly
- silly
- strange
- safe
- good
- sunny
- little
- big
- friendly
- pretty
- ugly
- nice

WOW

BREAK } { UP } { STORY }

WORD PARTS TO USE

Some words are made up of two smaller words.
Read this story and fill in the missing word parts.

What does a cow_____ do on his birth_____?

(This true story was told by an old _____man

about a lazy cow _____ named _____poke.)

_____poke wakes up at _____rise, hungry

for _____fast. The cook serves him

pan_____, _____milk, and dough_____.

He goes out into the _____shine to do his chores.

He sees many _____flies, pretty yellow

_____cups, and _____pokes on _____back.

His friends yell, "To ____ is your _____day.

Would you like to play base_____, foot_____,

or basket_____?"

"Since it's my _____day," the _____boy

said, "I want to play _____shoes."

So that's what they did.

After a full day _____poke went to sleep at

_____set.

What does a cow_____ do on his birth_____?

Why, he gets a year older!

WORD PARTS TO USE

horse

boy

sun

cakes

slow

nuts

birth

day

break

ball

cow

butter

Extra Stuff) Illustrate a paragraph
from this story. 108

Tall Tales

CENTRAL PURPOSE:

Creative Expression

CENTER OBJECTIVES:

After completing the center activities the student should be able to:

(1)   write dialogue to complete a picture story.
(2)   complete a picture story creatively.
(3)   write an original story.

PROCEDURE:

1.   Place activity sheets, pencils, and dictionaries in the center. Place the title "A Crazy School Day" on an empty bulletin board near the center.

2.   Verbally introduce the center.

3.   Arrange time for discussion and evaluation of each activity and provide guidance and reinforcement as needed.

4.   Make provision for sharing completed stories in a group setting.

5.   Ask the student to add ideas to the bulletin board display.

Write what you think the people are saying in this story.

Use words and pictures to tell what could happen next in this story.

A "CRAZY" SCHOOL DAY

Write a story about the strange things that happened at school the day the teacher was absent.

_____

_____

_____

_____

_____

_____

 Write a story about what will happen when the teacher comes back to school.

What's Your Line

CENTRAL PURPOSE:

Dialogue Development

CENTER OBJECTIVES:

After completing the center activities the student should
be able to:

(1) participate more spontaneously in telephone
conversations.

(2) express awareness of the dynamics of dialogue
associated with sales of consumer goods.

(3) enter creatively into "point of view" discussions.

PROCEDURE:

1. Place activity sheets, pencils, and resource
books in the center.

2. Lead a discussion of the importance of clear and
concise self-expression.

3. Explain each activity in as much detail as necessary
to enable the student to work independently.
Encourage the use of resource books for idea
clarification and vocabulary suggestions.

4. Arrange to give guidance and assistance and to
aid in ongoing evaluation.

5. Encourage extension of center ideas to culminate
in group discussion and/or creative dramatics.

HOT LINE

Create telephone conversations
for the situations given below.

SITUATION (The caller's task)	REACTION OF PERSON CALLED (Choose one for each situation)	WHAT NEXT?
You are late to dinner...	(a) The food is burned and you are angry. (b) You have already eaten.	......
Invite a friend to a party that is only for your best friends.	(a) After invitation is made, you tell him that he called the wrong number, but that you want to come. (b) You don't want to come.	......
Call a friend for a homework assignment.	(a) You get the directions mixed up. (b) You didn't get the assignment either, but you don't want to admit it.	......
Order a birthday cake with green frosting, purple roses, 100 yellow candles, with "Happy Birthday" written in gray.	(a) You can't get the directions straight. (b) You don't have any cakes and you try to sell caller a pie.	......
You are the teacher and call a parent to tell about child's bad grade.	(a) You are the child and you make excuses as to why the parent can't come to the phone. (b) You are the parent and think the grade is unfair.	......
You are lost and need directions to a friend's house.	(a) You can't figure out where the caller is calling from. (b) Give directions and insist the caller tell them back to you.	......

114

NOW

Choose a topic and take a side.
Are you "pro" (for) or "con"
(against) the statement?
Think of the arguments for
your side of the situation.

One example for each position
statement is given.

1. Debate the issue with yourself.   (Think of possible
   arguments for both sides.)
2. Debate with a friend.
3. Debate in teams.

SITUATION	POSITION 1 (Pro)	POSITION 2 (Con)
Concrete is better than grass on the playground.	(a) You don't have to cut grass. (b) (c)	(a) If you fall, you'll hurt yourself. (b) (c)
Astroturf should be put on the ball field.	(a) It would keep the field dry and free of mud. (b) (c)	(a) You can't run as fast. (b) (c)
Motorcycles are dangerous.	(a) You don't have the same protection as in a car. (b) (c)	(a) A special driver's license means you have the necessary skills. (b) (c)
Money should be spent for sending men to the moon.	(a) We should discover new frontiers. (b) (c)	(a) Money should be spent for people who are hungry. (b) (c)

Extra Stuff — Debate other topics of interest.
Suggestions: TV is more informative than radio.
Summer is more fun than winter.
Reading is still important even
though we have television.

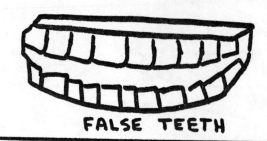

FALSE TEETH

Be a super salesman! Try to sell these products to a friend.

Things to include in your
SUPER SALES PITCH:

1. What it can be used for _____

   _____

2. Why it is worth buying _____

   _____

3. Why the buyer really needs the product _____

4. Draw pictures or find them in magazines to enhance your sale.

AN EMPTY BOX

CLOTHES THAT DON'T FIT

BROKEN GLASSES

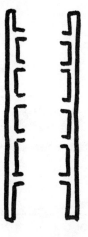

A LADDER WITH NO STEPS

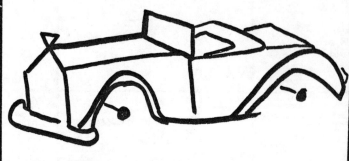

A CAR WITHOUT WHEELS

A TABLE WITH A BROKEN LEG

More Products to Sell:

A Flat Tire
A Bucket with a Hole in it
A Pen with No Ink
Two Left Shoes
Play Money

A Set of Broken Dishes
A Burned Out Electric Light Bulb
A Brown Sock and a White Sock
A Key that Has No Lock
A Ticket to Last Week's Show

World of Words

CENTRAL PURPOSE:

Creative Word Usage

CENTER OBJECTIVES:

After completing the center activities the student should be able to:

(1)　express awareness of word meanings.
(2)　use words creatively.
(3)　develop a story with plot and sequence based on specific word usage.

PROCEDURES:

1.　Place activity sheets, dictionaries, pencils, construction paper, and felt tip markers in the center.

2.　Verbally introduce the center.

3.　Focus individual and group discussion on words being used and develop chart or chalkboard word lists.

4.　Arrange time for discussion and ongoing evaluation of each activity.

5.　Encourage the student to use construction paper and felt tip markers to make covers for a booklet entitled "World of Words" to contain the completed activities.

CREATE A "B" STORY

bee

book

Write a story using as many of these "B" words as you can.

(For example: A big bee buzzed by Betsy's basket.)

bandaid

bicycle

bucket

bounce

ball

bandit

bunch of bananas

basket

bat

bump

More words to use:

boy	buy	blue	beautiful	bang	big	buzzing	bright
but	blouse	black	bored	brother	bed	bent	bite
baby	back	book	box	because	bring	brown	by
best	better	birthday					

NOW

118

CREATE A "P" STORY

Write a story using as many of these "P" words as you can.

(For example: Patsy planned a picnic party...")

pumpkin

pretzel

prize

penny

present

pie

potato

people

pleased

pickle

peanuts

popcorn

More words to use:

party   pen   pass   past   pick   play   pay   pet   pretty

pull   pink   pants   paper   pin   pan   pot   purple   pig

plan   plane   pack   prune   pain

CREATE A "T" STORY

Write a story using as many of these "T" words as you can.

(For example: An elephant tripped over his trunk
and tumbled on his tail...)

tomato

tripping

thumb

toe

teacher

tail

two together

think

town

train TOOT!

More words to use:

travel	tool	turn	three	ten	trouble	tree	try
table	tiny	truck	tip	top	the	to	them	they
there	this	that	thin	take	talk	took	today

120

Select one of the following letters and develop your own activity sheet.
Be sure to include the giant letter, illustrations and words to use. Write
your story.

C   R   G   S   K   N   V

More words to use:

Review the four stories you have just written. Select your favorite and illustrate it here.

Title: _____

Make a list of ten words from your story that you know how to spell and pronounce correctly and that you would like to use in conversation with your friends.

1. _____   6. _____

2. _____   7. _____

3. _____   8. _____

4. _____   9. _____

5. _____   10. _____

POW

Dizzy Descriptions

CENTRAL PURPOSE:

Descriptive Words

CENTER OBJECTIVES:

After completing this center the student should be able to:

(1) use descriptive words with understanding.
(2) associate descriptive words with pictures and emotions.
(3) use descriptive words in sentence construction.

PROCEDURE:

1. Place activity sheets and pencils in the center.

2. Provide motivation and develop readiness for the center by discussing the use of descriptive words, and how they make speaking and writing more interesting.

3. Explain center activities to enable the student to work as independently as possible.

4. Arrange time for evaluation of completed activities.

5. Make provision for filing or displaying completed activities.

Fill the hand with words that describe the way things feel to the touch.

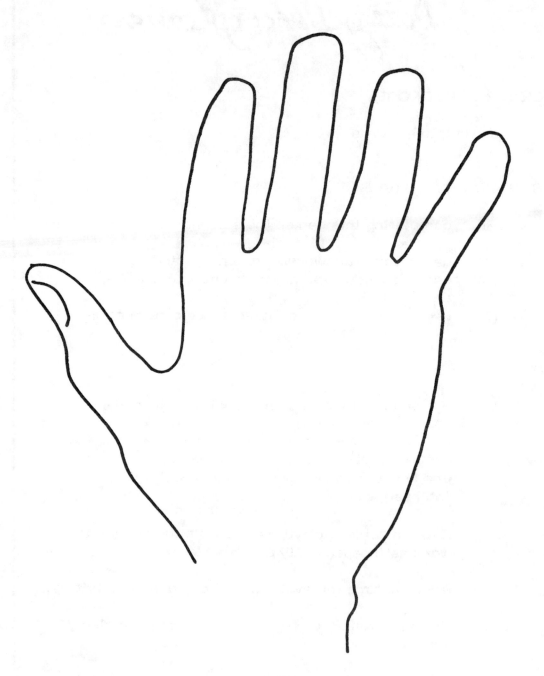

Write a descriptive word for each of these things:

sandpaper _____   kitten _____

cotton _____   broken glass _____

wet rock _____   rain _____

knife _____   paper bag _____

glue _____   marshmallow _____

NOW

Complete these words that describe feelings.

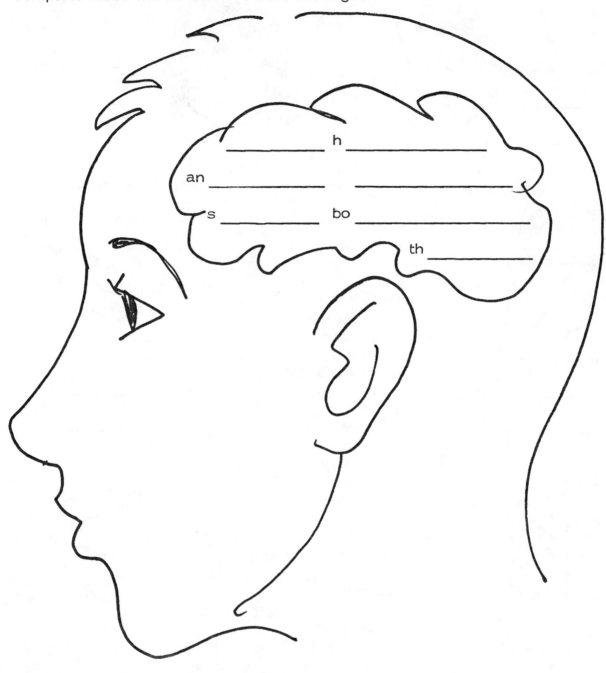

_____ h _____

an _____   _____

s _____   bo _____

th _____

List four thoughts that make you happy:

_____   _____

_____   _____

List four thoughts that make you sad:

_____   _____

_____   _____

_____ _____
_____ _____
_____ _____

Match these words and pictures.
Write each word next to the face it best
describes.

blushing
angry
shy
tired
surprised
furious
bored
pleased
unhappy
sly
questioning
sleepy
sneaky
happy
wondering
crying
bashful
sad
thinking
shocked
glad
frightened
annoyed
shifty

_____ _____
_____ _____
_____ _____

_____ _____
_____ _____
_____ _____

128

Homonym Review

CENTRAL PURPOSE:

Using Homonyms

CENTER OBJECTIVES:

After completing this center the student should be able to:

(1) recognize words that sound alike but have different meanings.
(2) use homonyms meaningfully.
(3) use homonyms to express creative thoughts.

PROCEDURE:

1. Place activity sheets, pencils, dictionaries, construction paper, and crayons in the center.

2. Verbally introduce the center.

3. Arrange time for discussion and ongoing evaluation of each activity.

4. Make provision for sharing completed activity sheets in a small group setting.

5. Ask the student to use construction paper to make a folder for the completed activity sheets before they are taken home to be shared with family members.

Circle the word pictured in each box. Write a sentence using the circled word.

---

knows

nose

_____

_____

ate   eight

8

_____

_____

two

too

to

2

_____

_____

some   sum

$4+5=?$

_____

_____

flower

flour

_____

_____

sew

so

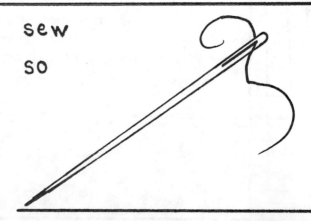

_____

_____

Circle the word pictured in each box. Write a sentence using the circled word.

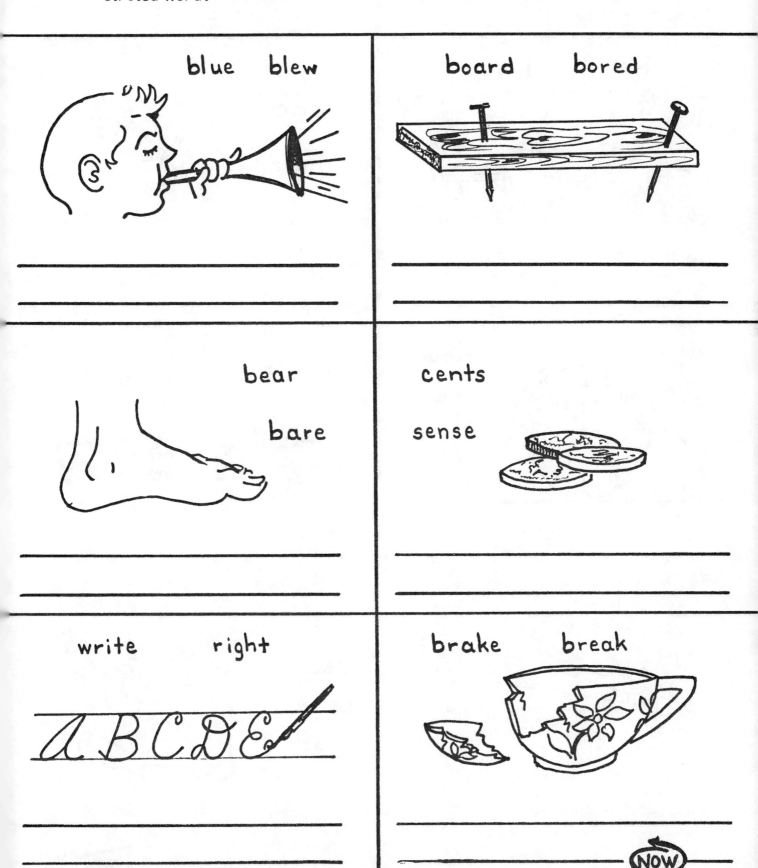

blue   blew

board   bored

bear

bare

cents

sense

write   right

brake   break

NOW

Circle the word pictured in each box. Write a sentence using the
circled word.

lie   lye

hare

hair

hour

our

heard   herd

cite

site

sight

sees

seize

seas

132

WOW

Find these words in the puzzle and circle them:

an
too
to
tall
two
look
like
toe
not

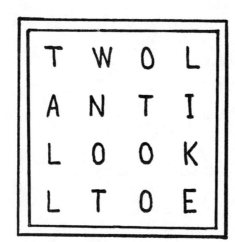

Extra Stuff → TO , TOO, and TWO are words that sound the same but have different meanings.

A.   Circle the correct word to complete each sentence.

1.   I went (to, too, two) the zoo.

2.   I have (to, too, two) hands.

3.   I ate (to, too, two) much candy.

B.   Complete this story by writing in the correct word – TO, TOO, or TWO – in each blank.

I went _____ the store _____ buy _____ apples.

The grocer gave four apples _____ me. I told

him that he gave _____ many apples _____ me.

He gave me _____ more than the _____ apples I

wanted _____ buy.

Choose the correct word for each sentence.

The story was written _____ Mark Twain.
(by, buy)

Roy _____ his friend.
(seas, sees, seize)

Tom goes _____ school.
(to, two, too)

Did you ever see a big brown _____ asleep in a bed?
(bare, bear)

All our friends are _____.
(hear, here)

The _____ for the race was a rough one.
(course, coarse)

Jan _____ the bed.
(made, maid)

The kittens' _____ to come inside were ignored.
(please, pleas)

Joe and Tom went to _____ house.
(there, their, they're)

Jack went fishing with his rod and _____.
(real, reel)

There were _____ pieces of cake left on the plate.
(four, for)

It was Jill's turn to _____ the drum.
(beet, beat)

Tony needed to repair the emergency _____ on his car.
(break, brake)

The _____ of the new shopping center was on the corner.
(cite, site, sight)

Bob was so _____ that he fell asleep.
(board, bored)

Extra Stuff) Write sentences with the words not used above.

134

Joe's Diner

CENTRAL PURPOSE:

Word Discrimination

CENTER OBJECTIVES:

After completing this center the student should be able to:

(1)   identify like words.
(2)   identify like phrases.
(3)   identify like sentences.
(4)   distinguish between like and unlike sentences.

PROCEDURE:

1.   Place activity sheets, pencils, drawing paper, and crayons in the center.

2.   Verbally introduce the center, giving examples and detailed instructions for completing the activities.

3.   Arrange time for ongoing evaluation and given reinforcement as needed.

4.   Encourage the student to use drawing paper and crayons to pictorially portray his interpretation of "Joe's Diner".

5.   Make provision for sharing completed activities in a group setting.

The words in the boxes are listed in Joe's Menu.
Circle the word in each line that is the same as
the word in the box.

ham	bam	ham	tum	hum
jam	jim	jam	jan	tam
bread	head	bred	dread	bread
pear	pair	par	pear	peer
cake	rake	make	sake	cake
bean	bean	dean	been	bear
corn	cone	corn	come	scorn
meat	neat	moat	meat	meet
candy	andy	candy	sandy	canny
fish	dish	fist	fish	wish
grape	group	grape	drape	grate

 Make sentences using the words in the boxes.

NOW

136

Cross out the "speciality" on each line that is different from the other two.

hot cakes	hot cokes	hot cakes
fig pudding	fig pudding	big pudding
freed eggs	fried eggs	fried eggs
bean soup	bean soup	bear soup
french fries	french tries	french fries
cornbread	cornbread	corndread
cheese pie	chess pie	chess pie
fresh fruit	french fruit	fresh fruit
orange juice	orange juice	orange truce
hat dogs	hot dogs	hot dogs
milk shake	milk shade	milk shake
pork chops	pork chops	pork shops
ham steak	ham stake	ham steak
chicken soup	chicken soup	chicken coup
battered toast	buttered toast	buttered toast

Joe makes a list of things he must remember to do for his restaurant.
Circle the matching phrase for the one in each box.

set the table	sat the table set the table set the lable
pour the tea	pour the tea poor the tea pure the tea
wash the pot	wish the pot wash the got wash the pot
heat the grill	heat the girl beat the grill heat the grill
mop the floor	mop the floor map the floor nap the floor
dry the fork	dry the fort dry the fork pry the fork
cook the food	cook the food cool the food cook the foot

WOW

138

Joe made a list of the things he did <u>not</u> want to do in his restaurant. Circle the two phrases in each box that are the same.

spill the milk
spell the milk
spill the milk
spoil the milk

break the cup
brake the cup
break the cap
break the cup

trip the winter
trip the waiter
trip the waiter
drip the waiter

drop the tray
drop the tray
drip the tray
drop the trap

burn the beans
barn the beans
burn the beans
turn the bears

Extra Stuff Using the phrases that you circled, make a list of the things Joe did not want to do.

slip on the map
slip on the mop
slap on the mop
slip on the mop

139

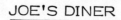

Have you ever had dinner at Joe's Diner?
The cook looks like he likes good food.
I ate the food the cook cooks. His food
does not look good. His food does not
taste good. There must be a finer diner
for dinner.

Circle the sentence in each box that matches a sentence in the story.

The cook looks like he likes good food.
The cook looks like he like good food.
The look cooks like he likes good food.

There must be a finer dinner for diner.
There must be a finer diner for dinner.
There must be a diner finer for dinner.

His food dose not look good.
His good does not look food.
His food does not look good.

Have you never had dinner at Joe's Diner?
Have you ever had dinner in Joe's Diner?
Have you ever had dinner at Joe's Diner?

I ate the food the cook cooked.
I ate the food the cook cooks.
I ate the cook the food cooks.

Extra Stuff

Circle all of the a's on the page.
Cross out all of the e's.

Ladder Leaders

CENTRAL PURPOSE:

Vowel Discrimination

CENTER OBJECTIVES:

After completing the center activities the student should be able to:

(1)   identify long vowel sounds.
(2)   identify short vowel sounds.
(3)   distinguish between long and short vowel sounds.

PROCEDURE:

1.   Place activity sheets, pencils, manila folders, and felt tip markers in the center.

2.   Verbally introduce the center.

3.   Arrange for a free traffic flow and flexibility in scheduling to allow students to work together to complete the activities.

4.   Make provision for ongoing evaluation and give as much immediate feedback as possible.

5.   Ask the student to use felt tip markers to illustrate and label the manila folders to contain the completed activity sheets for future use.

Read each word and decide if the vowel sound is long or short. Write the word in the correct space in the long or short vowel ladder. (A clue letter is given for each word.)

WORDS: late   lamp   ant   taste
           ate   eight   bat   man

Long A Vowel Ladder

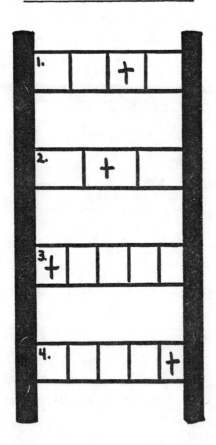

Short A Vowel Ladder

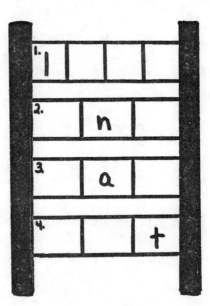

To solve each code, find the letters you have written in the numbered ladder boxes.

LONG Ā CODE

The opposite of early

is ___ ___ ___ ___ .
   1   2   3   4

SHORT Ă CODE

A baby sheep is

a ___ ___ ___ ___ .
   1   2   3   4

142

Read each word and decide if the vowel sound is long or short. Write the word in the correct spaces in the long or short vowel ladder. (A clue letter is given for each word.)

WORDS: bead   bread   set   seat
           feed   fed   feel   fell

Long E Vowel Ladder

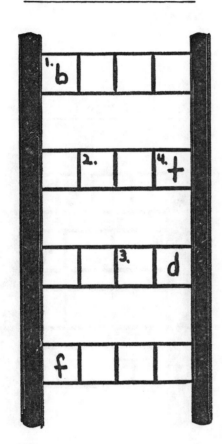

Short E Vowel Ladder

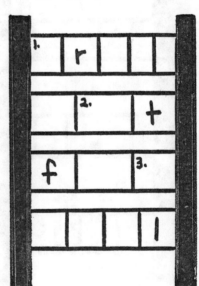

To solve each code, find the letters you have written in the numbered ladder boxes.

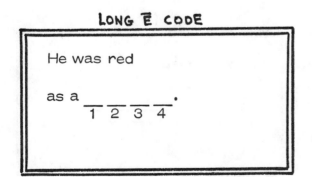

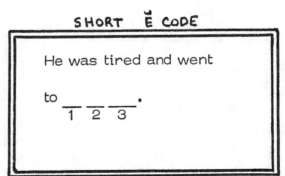

LONG Ē CODE

He was red

as a ___ ___ ___ ___ .
     1   2   3   4

SHORT Ĕ CODE

He was tired and went

to ___ ___ ___ .
   1   2   3

143

Read each word and decide if the vowel sound is long or short. Write the word in the correct spaces in the short or long vowel ladders. (A clue letter is given for each word.)

WORDS: pick   ice   hid   hide
        sight   gift   white sit

Long I Vowel Ladder

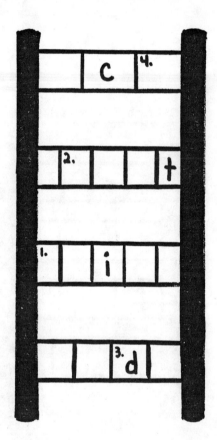

Short I Vowel Ladder

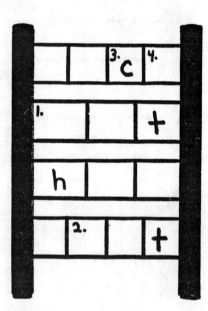

To solve each code, find the letters you have written in the numbered ladder boxes.

LONG I CODE

The opposite of

narrow is $\frac{}{1}\ \frac{}{2}\ \frac{}{3}\ \frac{}{4}$.

SHORT I CODE

The opposite of

healthy is $\frac{}{1}\ \frac{}{2}\ \frac{}{3}\ \frac{}{4}$.

Read each word and decide if the vowel sound is long or short. Write the word in the correct spaces in the long or short vowel ladder. (A clue letter is given for each word.)

WORDS: hop   not   hope   rod
               note   toe   road   tot

Long O Vowel Ladder

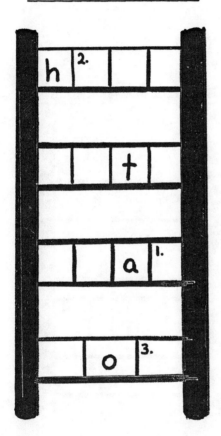

Short O Vowel Ladder

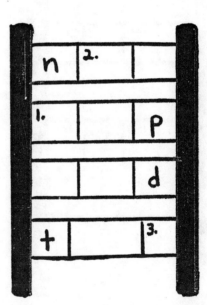

To solve each code, find the letters you have written in the numbered ladder boxes.

LONG Ō CODE	SHORT Ŏ CODE
A female deer is a ___ ___ ___ . 1 2 3	The opposite of cold is ___ ___ ___ . 1 2 3

145

Read each word and decide if the vowel sound is long or short. Write the word in the correct spaces in the short or long vowel ladders. (A clue letter is given for each word.)

WORDS: tub   shut   cube   tube
          suit   cub   rule   rug

Long U Vowel Ladder

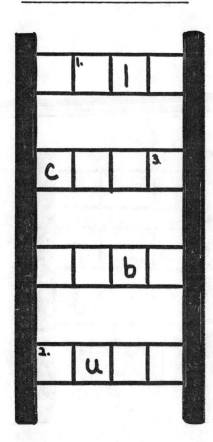

Short U Vowel Ladder

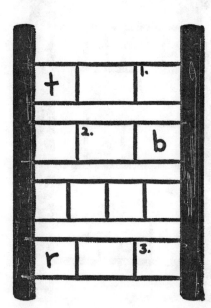

To solve each code, find the letters you have written in the numbered ladder boxes.

LONG U CODE	SHORT U CODE
A tool is a thing to ___ ___ ___. 　　　　1　2　3	She was snug as a ___ ___ ___ in a rug. 1　2　3

146

Moving On

CENTRAL PURPOSE:

Verb Usage

CENTER OBJECTIVES:

After completing this center the student should be able to:

(1) use action words correctly.
(2) change verbs from present to past tense.
(3) use verbs creatively to express original thoughts.

PROCEDURE:

1. Place activity sheets, pencils, dictionaries, and extra paper in the center.

2. Verbally introduce the center and devote as much time as necessary to the development of understanding of verbs and their usage.

3. Arrange for two students to work together to complete the activities and to "check" each other's completed work.

4. Make provision for filing or displaying completed activity sheets.

Look at the picture carefully.

Discuss what is happening in the picture with a friend.

List five action words that can be used to describe what is happening in the picture.

Action Words

_____

_____

_____

_____

_____

Compare your list of words
with your friend's list.

Write an action word to complete each sentence.

Rewrite each sentence and change the verbs to past tense.

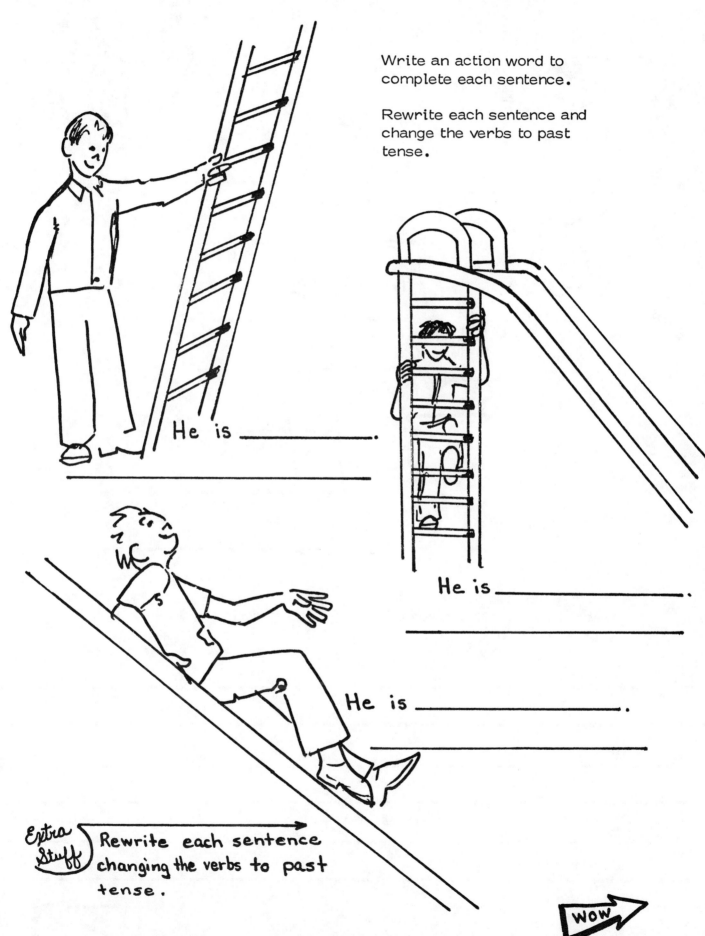

He is _____.

_____

He is _____.

_____

He is _____.

_____

Extra Stuff ⟶ Rewrite each sentence changing the verbs to past tense.

WOW ⟶

149

Write an action word on each line below.

Write a creative story including something the boy is doing, something he did in the past, and something he plans to do in the future. Share your story with a friend.

PAST: _____

_____

PRESENT: _____

_____

FUTURE: _____

_____

Read each sentence to a friend.
Ask the friend to change the verb to past tense and repeat the sentence. The verbs are underlined and the correct answer is given at the end of each sentence.

Example: You say, "John <u>walks</u>."
Your friend should say, "John <u>walked</u>."

1. Sue <u>talks</u>. (Sue talked.)

2. Tim <u>jumps</u>. (Tim jumped.)

3. Joe <u>hops</u>. (Joe hopped.)

4. Bob <u>plays</u> ball. (Bob played ball.)

5. Barbara <u>looks</u> at television. (Barbara looked at television.)

6. Mary <u>listens</u> to Jane. (Mary listened to Jane.)

7. Sam <u>carries</u> the box. (Sam carried the box.)

8. Jason <u>eats</u> bread. (Jason ate bread.)

9. Tom <u>sits</u> on the chair. (Tom sat on the chair.)

10. Jennifer <u>runs</u> to school. (Jennifer ran to school.)

11. David <u>comes</u> to supper. (David came to supper.)

12. Jean <u>sees</u> the book. (Jean saw the book.)

13. Sally <u>writes</u> a letter. (Sally wrote a letter.)

14. Henry <u>goes</u> to the show. (Henry went to the show.)

Extra Stuff → Read the sentences again. This time ask your friend to make them into sentences using the future tense of the verbs.
For example: (you) "John walks."
(friend) "John will walk."

Change each verb from present tense to past tense. Write the past tense of the verbs in the puzzle boxes.

Across:

1. take
3. eat
5. is
7. come
9. do
11. run

Down:

2. know
4. ask
6. use
8. give
10. drink

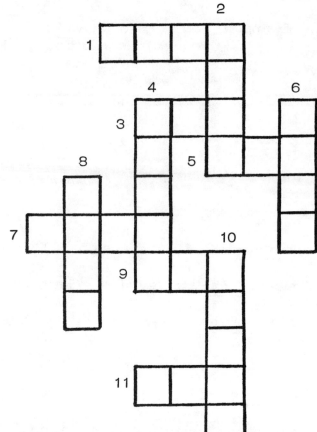

Extra Stuff — Change the present tense verbs to past tense and use them to work the puzzle.

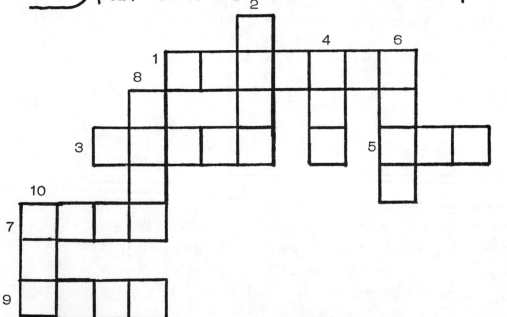

Across:

1. bring
3. find
5. lead
7. are
9. pay

Down:

2. sell
4. get
6. tell
8. go
10. weep

Name Dropping

CENTRAL PURPOSE:

Using Nouns and Pronouns

CENTER OBJECTIVES:

After completing this center the student should be able
to:

(1)   recognize and use nouns.
(2)   recognize and use pronouns.
(3)   use possessive pronouns.

PROCEDURE:

1.   Place activity sheets, pencils, and dictionaries
       in the center.

2.   Verbally introduce the center activities and review
       the definitions for nouns and pronouns and rules
       related to their use.

3.   Encourage the student to complete the activities
       as independently as possible. Provide time for
       ongoing guidance and evaluation.

4.   Encourage the student to take the completed
       activity sheets home to share with family members
       or friends.

Look at the pictures and write their names in the correct numbered spaces in the puzzle.

Nouns to use:

		car		
book	chair	bird	horse	girl
table	bear	pencil	ball	boy

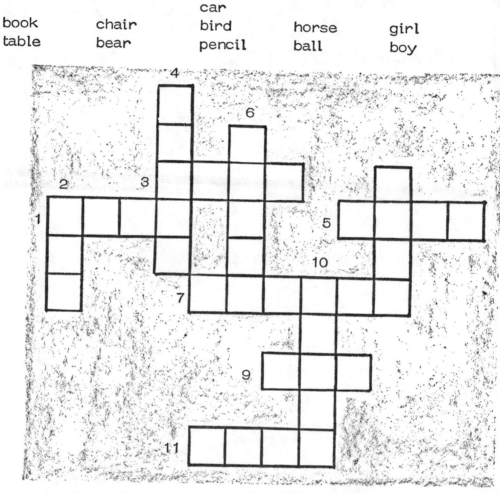

Across:
1   3   5   7   9   11

Down:
2   4   6   8   10

NOW

Find the pronouns in this puzzle and circle them.

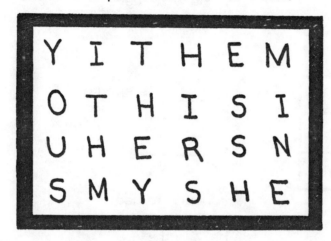

Pronoun Clues: Complete these sentences with the correct pronoun.
Find the pronouns in the puzzle.

1. I love y __ __.

2. This towel is hers. This one is h __ __.

3. That bicycle is yours. This one is m __ __ __.

4. They went to the party. I went with t __ __ __.

5. He wears shirts. S __ __ wears skirts.

6. That book is yours. T __ __ __ one is mine.

7. She is a girl. H __ is a boy.

8. The boys went to the movies. T __ __ __ had a good time.

9. __ love you.

10. The blue car is his. The pink one is h __ __ __.

11. I lost my hat. Do you know where i __ is?

155

Find the correct pronoun for each blank.
Write the pronouns in the puzzle boxes.

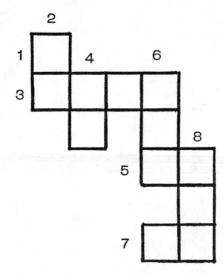

Across:

1. _____ (one letter meaning me)
3. _____ are talking
5. He will see _____.
7. _____ are working the puzzle together.

Down:

2. _____ is spring.
4. _____ is a boy.
6. _____ are working with your friend.
8. _____ is a girl.

Pronouns to use:

he	they
she	I
it	us
we	you

Extra Stuff Fill in the blanks with the correct possessive pronouns. Use the pronouns to work this puzzle.

Across:

1. I use __ __ pencil.
3. We go to __ __ __ own house.
5. They go to __ __ __ __ __ own house.
7. He reads __ __ __ own book.

Down:

2. In fall the tree loses __ __ __ leaves.
4. You use __ __ __ __ own pencil.
6. She uses __ __ __ own pencil.

156

Perfect Ending

CENTRAL PURPOSE:

Using Suffixes

CENTER OBJECTIVES:

After completing this center the student should be able to:

(1)   recognize suffixes within words.
(2)   add suffixes to root words to make new words.
(3)   recognize and use root words.
(4)   alter story plots by changing the suffixes of given root words.

PROCEDURE:

1.   Place activity sheets, pencils, and dictionaries in the center.

2.   Verbally introduce the center, giving examples and explaining instructions for completion of each activity.

3.   Arrange time for ongoing evaluation and give reinforcement as needed.

4.   Make provision for sharing completed activities in a small group setting.

Help the director write his opening night "pep-talk" to the actors.
Write the correct root word and suffix in each blank.

Root words to use: Suffixes:

    power   –ness (the state of being)
    success   –ful (full of)
    happy   –er (one who...)
    care   –ors (ones who...)
    dark
    act   Opening Night
    wonder
    kind
    sing
    help
    direct

It will be a _____ day for all the _____.
            (full of wonder)   (ones who act)

Be _____ to learn your lines. Be _____ to the
   (full of care)   (full of help)

other _____.
    (ones who act)

When the lights are out be _____ not to fall in the
                       (full of care)

_____. Be _____ to the _____.
(state of being dark)   (full of help)   (ones who act)

_____ will help you find _____.
(the state of being kind)   (the state of being happy)

If you are in the group of _____, watch the musical
                 (ones who sing)

_____.
(one who directs)

I know your show will be a hit! When the play is over you will

know what a _____ feeling it is to be _____.
      (full of power)   (full of success)

Read this story and circle the words that have the following endings:

-est   -ward   -ed   -ing

BACKWARD MOVES

The funniest movie I ever saw was about a girl who did everything backward. She would go to bed in the morning and get up at night. She brushed her teeth before eating candy and washed her hands before playing with clay. When it was raining she would wait until she was inside the house to put on her raincoat. She read her book backward and answered the last question of a test first. She put her dress over her coat and wore her socks over her shoes. The only thing she would do frontward was to back up!

Write the base word for each word circled in the story:

1. _____   6. _____

2. _____   7. _____

3. _____   8. _____

4. _____   9. _____

5. _____   10. _____

Extra Stuff → Write your own story about someone doing things backward and illustrate it.

Rewrite this soap opera script. Using the suffixes -ful or - less,
change the ending of each underlined word so that the script makes sense.

Mary: Oh, Charles, this is a joyless occasion. You
        have returned home! The time you were gone seemed
        endful.

Charles: Mary, my Mary, you are so thoughtless to care for
        my safe homecoming.

Mary: Charles, you are so fearful to travel alone to the
        supermarket. You are indeed a powerless person!

Charles: It was nothing. I just had to be watchless of the
        careful shoppers and their grocery carts.

Mary: You must be very tired. I hope you have a restless
        night. What can I do to be helpless?

Charles: I am thankless that I have such a dutiless wife to care
        for me. You can bring my colorless slippers for my
        sore feet.

Mary: Oh, Charles, you are so good to make me feel so useless!

Extra Stuff) Write a soap opera script and act it out with a friend. WOW

Fill in the blanks by adding the correct suffix to the word at the end of each sentence. Write the changed words in the numbered puzzle boxes.

Suffixes to use: −ly   −ward   −less
−ful   −ness   −ion

Across:

1. The movie was full of _____ and adventure. (act)
3. Jim is always so happy and _____. (cheer)
5. The truck rolled _____ down the hill. (back)
7. Thank you for your _____. (kind)
9. I felt so _____ when the kitten couldn't climb down the tree. (help)
11. That was a good answer for such a difficult _____. (quest)

Down:

2. You were very _____ to remember my birthday. (thought)
4. The light was so bright that we could _____ see what happened. (clear)
6. I look _____ to vacation time. (for)
8. A power failure left the city in total _____. (dark)
10. It was very _____ of you to leave your bicycle in the street. (care)
12. She smiled _____ and left the room. (sweet)

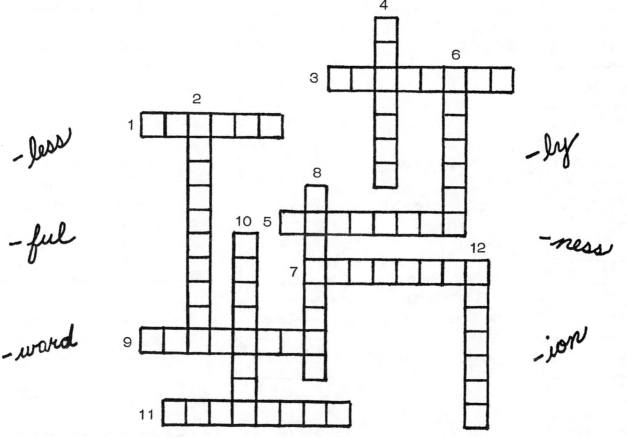

-less

-ful

-ward

-ly

-ness

-ion

POW

SUF ⟨ ⟨ FIX
WORD CONSTRUCTION

Make new words by finding a suffix for each root word. Check your words in the dictionary and define them.

ROOT WORDS	(SUFFIX MEANINGS)	SUFFIX	NEW WORDS
pay			
drain	(full of)	-ful	_____
front	(act or condition)	-ion	_____
clear	(act of; group of)	-age	_____
allow	(quality; degree)	-ity	_____
arm	(tends toward)	-ive	_____
cheer	(lacking)	-less	_____
care	(that can be)	-able	_____
help	(process; amount)	-ance	_____
wish	(able to be)	-ible	_____
collect	(state of)	-ness	_____
act	(state or result of happening)	-ing	_____
quest	(having happened)	-ed	_____
like	(change word into an adverb)	-ly	_____
real	(act of)	-ment	_____
effect	(person connected with something)	-er	_____
fruit	(one that does a thing)	-or	_____
ail	(in the direction of)	-ward	_____
fix			_____
sweet			_____

POW

Prefix Preview

CENTRAL PURPOSE:

Using Prefixes

CENTER OBJECTIVES:

After completing the center activities the student should be able to:

(1) add prefixes to root words to make new words.
(2) rewrite sentences to incorporate prefixes added to root words.
(3) alter story plots by adding prefixes to root words.

PROCEDURE:

1. Place activity sheets, pencils, dictionaries, construction paper, and scissors in the center.

2. Verbally introduce the center, giving examples and explaining instructions for completion of each activity.

3. Arrange time for ongoing evaluation and give reinforcement as needed.

4. Ask the student to use construction paper to make additional root words and prefixes to cut apart and make new words by using the prefix word construction activity page as a model.

5. Make provision for sharing rewritten stories in a group setting and for filing other completed activities.

Andy was <u>unhappy</u>.

She was <u>ungrateful</u> for many

things. She was <u>unhealthy</u>.

Her parents were <u>unkind</u>.

Her teacher was <u>unfair</u>. Her

classmates were <u>unfriendly</u>.

It's <u>unbelievable</u> that a girl

can be so <u>unlucky</u>!

Rewrite this story. Change "Unlucky Andy" to "Lucky Andy" by leaving off the prefix "un-" in the underlined words.

<u>LUCKY ANDY</u>

_____

_____

_____

_____

_____

_____

_____

_____

_____

_____

Rewrite the sentences. Change the meaning by adding prefixes to the underlined words.

The baseball player <u>planted</u> the flower <u>in</u> the <u>field</u>.

prefixes to use: | trans- | out- |

_____

_____

_____

_____

The boy was <u>lucky</u> because he counted the money <u>correctly</u>.

prefixes to use: | un- | in- |

_____

_____

_____

_____

_____

He wore his shirt <u>buttoned</u> because the party was <u>formal</u>.

prefixes to use: | un- | in- |

_____

_____

_____

_____

_____

When she <u>spelled</u> the word "right" on the test she felt <u>secure</u>.

prefixes to use: | mis- | in- |

_____

_____

_____

_____

_____

_____

Rewrite the sentences. Add the prefixes to the underlined words.

prefixes: tri- de-

He rode his cycle on a tour.

DETOUR

_____

prefixes: mis- un-

Sue understood because she was familiar with the information.

_____

prefixes: non- re-

This sentence was written so that it makes sense.

SENSE
SENSE NONSENSE

_____

prefixes: uni- re- ex-

Harry turned to the store to change his cycle.

STORE
EXCHANGE

_____

prefixes: pre- dis- in-

Due to his occupation with justice, he was trustful.

UNFAIR

_____

WOW

166

Repete the rebuilder has to redo everything. He rebuilds houses. He rehammers and renails every board. He replaces the carpets. He repaints the walls. He rehangs the wallpaper. He even replants the grass.

Repete wants to rebuild his bank account so he reapplies to be repaid in cash before all the work has been redone.

Would you repay Repete for all the work he has to redo?

. . .

Rewrite the story. Change Repete's name and the way he works by leaving off the prefix "re-" every time it appears in the story.

PETE THE BUILDER

POW

WORD CONSTRUCTION

Make new words by finding a prefix for each root word. Check your words in the dictionary and define them.

PREFIXES	(MEANINGS)	ROOT WORDS	NEW WORDS
bi-	(two)	trust	
		view	
con-	(with)	cycle	
		lay	
de-	(do the opposite)	tend	
		place	
dis-	(away from)	large	
en-	(to make)	joy	
		grown	
ex-	(out of)	cite	
		claim	
in-	(within)	form	
		like	
mis-	(wrong)	fit	
non-	(not, lack of)	take	
		sense	
pre-	(before)	vent	
pro-	(forward)	part	
re-	(again)	force	
un-	(not)	tract	

Rhyme Match

CENTRAL PURPOSE:

Using Rhyming Words

CENTER OBJECTIVES:

After completing the center the student should be able to:

(1)   recognize rhyming words.
(2)   make meaningful use of rhyming words.

PROCEDURE:

1.   Place activity sheets, pencils, extra paper, and crayons in the center.

2.   Play a rhyming word game as motivation for the center. Discuss activity sheets and give detailed instructions for their completion.

3.   Arrange time for guidance and ongoing evaluation.

4.   Make provision for filing completed activities.

Name the pictures in each box. Mark the two pictures that rhyme.

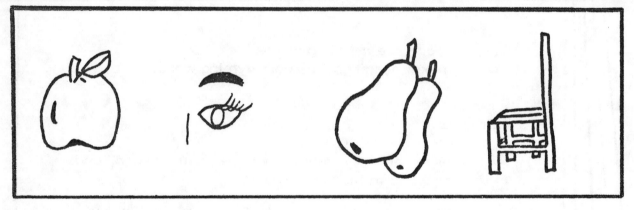

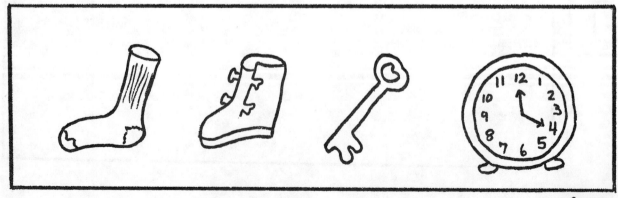

Look at the words at the bottom of the page and find a word that rhymes with each picture. Put the rhyming words in the correct puzzle boxes.

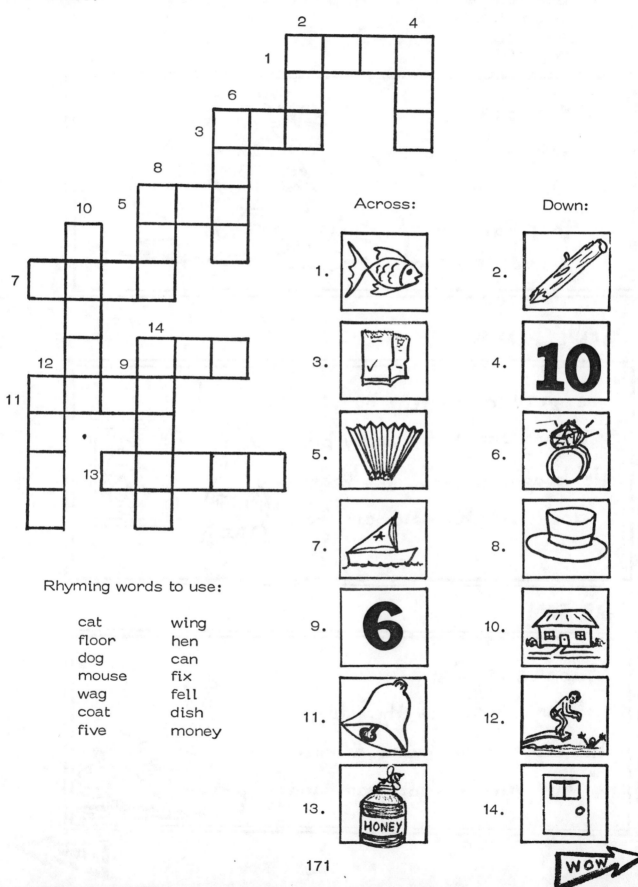

Across:

1.
3.
5.
7.
9.
11.
13.

Down:

2.
4.
6.
8.
10.
12.
14.

Rhyming words to use:

cat	wing
floor	hen
dog	can
mouse	fix
wag	fell
coat	dish
five	money

171

Read these rhyming stories.
Circle all the words that rhyme in each story.
Find the short a's and put a curved mark (ˇ) over the vowel. (For
      example: băt, Dăn, Săm)

A FAT CAT

A fat cat
    sat on my hat.
See how flat
    that fat cat
      made my hat!

DAN'S PLAN

The weather was very hot.
    Daring Dan had a dopey plan.
He bought a warm air heater
    and sold his cold air fan!

SAD SAM

Mad, sad Sam
    was playing in the sand.
He wanted to make a river,
    but all he got was land!

Read the rhyming stories.
Circle the words that rhyme in each story.
Find the short i's and put a curved mark (˘) over the vowel. (For
    example: kĭng, ĭtch)

KING, SING

The king found a wishing ring.
    He wished that he could sing.
What a silly, nilly thing —
    for a king to wish to sing!

WITCH, STITCH

There was a witch
    who liked to stitch.
She gave up her broom
    for a sewing room.

PIG WIG

Dick put a big wig
    on his pink pig.
It was a perfect fit
    But the pig didn't like it ...
                ONE BIT!

Read these rhyming stories. Follow the directions for each.

TEN IN A TENT

Circle all the words that rhyme with "Ken".
Underline the words that rhyme with "sent".
Cross out the words that rhyme with "led".
Find the short e's and put a curved mark (ᵕ) over the vowel.
   (For example: mĕn)

There were ten men in a crowded tent

So they went to find one to rent.

All they could find was an empty shed

So that is where five went to bed.

ROB'S JOB

Circle all the words that rhyme with "cob".
Underline the words that rhyme with "top".
Find the short o's and put a curved mark (ᵕ) over the vowel.
   (For example: pŏp)
Find the long o's and put a straight mark (−) over the vowel.
   (For example: ōne)

Pop owned a soda shop.

   He needed someone to mop.

So he hired a boy named Rob

   to do that special cleaning job.

Sound Off

CENTRAL PURPOSE:

Using Consonant Sounds and Blends

CENTER OBJECTIVES:

After completing the center the student should be able to:

(1) identify consonant sounds.
(2) supply consonant sounds to complete words.
(3) supply consonant blends to complete words used in context.

PROCEDURE:

1. Place activity sheets, pencils, and crayons in the center. Arrange a bulletin board display entitled "Sound-Off" and border it with consonant letters and blends cut from multi-colored construction paper.

2. Verbally introduce the center activities.

3. Arrange time for guidance and ongoing evaluation.

4. Ask students to work together in groups of three to complete activities. Arrange time blocks to allow for the "fun" type discussion that should be an important part of this center.

5. Make provision for filing completed activities for later referral.

Name the pictures in each box.

Mark the three pictures that have the same beginning sound.

NOW

Read this story to a friend. Read it again and ask him to fill in the missing sounds.

| b- | p- | or | f- |

We went to the stadium to see the team __lay __ase __all. The __atter at the __late __icked up the __at. He was so __at that when he threw the __all we saw him __all.

Extra Stuff

Complete the names of four other games that are played with a ball.

__asket__all   __ennis   __oot__all   __olf

177

Fill in these missing letters to complete this story.

There was a __asketball __layer named __aul who __ave the __ame his all. He had only one __ault and that was a shame. He brought a __ootball to the __asketball __ame. When he __ossed the __ootball in the __asket, he lost the __ame as well as his __ame.

Extra Stuff → Circle the words in the story that rhyme with "same".

178

Read this story to a friend. Read it again and ask him to fill in the missing sounds.

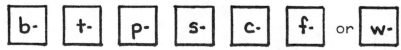

There are many ways to __ravel.
Some __eople like to fly on a __lane.
Some like to ride on a __rain.
__ailors like __oats and __hips.
Other folks like to drive in a
__ar or take a __us. Some of us
just like to use our __eet and
__alk!

Extra Stuff) Complete these transportation words.

b_____   c_____   p_____

t_____   s_____   b_____

Use these word endings to complete this story:

-ug   -ig   or   -ag

There was a b__ ugly b__
who lived in a paper b__ .
He jumped out of the b__,
ran over a dish r__ and
fell on the r__ .

Don't you wish you could be
as happy as that b__ ugly
b__ sn__ in the r__?

Extra Stuff Write a poem in the space below.
Use these words:
    pig   tag   dug
    wig   wag   tug

180

Use these letter combinations to complete
the words in this story:

th   dr   or   ck

___in, ___irsty Ru___ found
the pa___ to the Sna___ Sha___
owned by Ja___. By the time
she got ___ere her mou___
was so ___y ___at she ordered
___ree ___ings to ___ink. She
also asked for ___ree more
___ings to put in her sa___
for an afternoon sna___.

Extra Stuff ──────────────────────▶

List three things that Ruth could
have in her snack sack.

_____

_____

_____

Use these letter combinations to complete the questions below:

sh- ch- sw- scr- bl- cr- cl- qu- or fr-

Have you heard:

___ickens ___ucking?

___uebirds ___irping?

___ogs ___oaking?

___imming ducks ___acking?

___eep ___eating?

hungry babies ___ying?

___ildren ___outing and ___eaming?

Vowel Mixer

CENTRAL PURPOSE:

Using Vowel Sounds

CENTER OBJECTIVES:

After completing the center the student should
be able to:

(1) select vowels to complete words.
(2) add "e" to words to change short vowel sounds to
long vowel sounds.
(3) identify words with long vowel sounds.

PROCEDURE:

1. Place activity sheets, pencils, and art supplies
in the center.

2. Verbally introduce the center and explain the
directions for each activity.

3. Arrange to give guidance and assistance and to
aid in ongoing evaluation.

4. Make provision for filing or displaying completed
activities.

On this page are phrases from some recipe directions. Find and circle the correct word to complete the directions by using the hint at the end of each line.

                  cup

u   1.   Use one   sugar. (Hint: a word with a "u" like in duck)

                  cube

               ripe

i   2.   Use   fruit. (Hint: a word with an "i" like in pie)

              picked

            Bake

a   3.   for twenty minutes. (Hint: a word with an "A" like in make)

            Pat

              hot

o   4.   Pour   juice over the duck. (Hint: a word with an "o"

           orange   like in box)

            Pop

o   5.   corn over hot fire. (Hint: a word with an "o" like in bone)

           Roast

            Heat

e   6.   the chicken parts. (Hint: a word with an "e" like in feed)

            Wet

                cheese

e   7.   Chop the   well. (Hint: a word with an "e" like in fed)

              egg

              cake

a   8.   Place   in pan. (Hint: a word with an "a" like in fat)

            ham

            Use

u   9.   a large piece of meat. (Hint: a word with a "u" like in pure)

           Cut

               limes

i 10.   Use fresh   . (Hint: a word with an "i" like in fix)

              milk

Someone took everything out of the kitchen cabinet. Place the above items back in the cabinet by writing their names on the proper shelf.

Items that have the "a" sound as in ham

Items that have the "e" sound as in hen

Items that have the "i" sound as in pig

Items that have the "o" sound as in mop

Items that have the "u" sound as in duck

185

Complete these words by writing in the missing vowels.

m __ s t   br __ w n   j __ m p   w __ 1 k

pr __ t t y   b l __ c k   h __ d   br __ n g

s __ y   w h __ t e   c __ r r y   k __ n d

t h __ s   h __ r   l __ n g   w h __ t

h __ m   m __ c h   h __ r t   t h __ m

s h __ w   h __ m   t r __

__ l d   t w __   h __ l p

w __   b __   s t __ p

__ m   __ r   h __

__ p

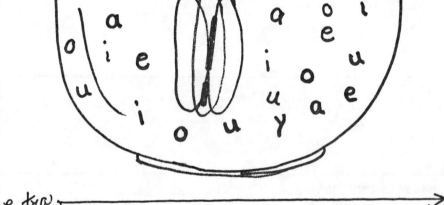

See how many words you can make by adding different vowels to these incomplete words.

n __ w   w __ l l   c __ t   h __ l d

s __ w   b __ t   f __ 1 1   t __ n

w __ n t   g __ t   g r __ w   b __ g

w __ s h   t __ p   __ n   s h __ 1 1

t h __ n k   h __ m   p __ t   w __ n

__ t   __ s   f __ r   m __

WOW

Rewrite each sentence. Add an "e" to the end of the underlined word. This will change the short vowel to a long vowel sound and make a new word. Circle the sentence which best describes the picture.

Bill put on his <u>cap</u>.

_____

Sally put a bandage on her <u>cut</u> finger.

_____

Please, don't <u>mop</u> around my desk.

_____

He walked with a <u>can</u> in his hand.

_____

<u>Tap</u> your foot on the floor.

_____

Tom's baby brother was left in his <u>car</u>.

_____

It was his <u>fat</u> that got him into trouble.

_____

<u>Tim</u> flies.

_____

Rewrite this story in the space below. Add the missing vowels.

Th__ l_st d__y of sch__ __l is a
h__ppy d__y.   Th__ s__mm__r m__nths
__re h__ppy d__ys of pl__y and no
sch__ __l w__rk.   St__d__nts w__sh
v__c__t__on c__uld l__st __ll ye__r,
b__t aft__r a l__ng s__mm__r th__y
s__em gl__d to g__t b__ck to th__
b__ __ks.

_____

_____

_____

_____

_____

_____

_____

_____

_____

_____

Word Hook-Up

CENTRAL PURPOSE:

Compound Word Usage

CENTER OBJECTIVES:

After completing the center activities the student should be able to:

(1)   make compound words from two small words.
(2)   associate compound words and pictures.
(3)   use compound words meaningfully.

PROCEDURE:

1.   Place activity sheets, pencils, and dictionaries in the center.

2.   Verbally introduce the center.

3.   Arrange conference time for discussion and evaluation of each completed activity and provide additional reinforcement as needed.

4.   Make provision for filing or displaying completed activity sheets.

5.   Ask the student to use the dictionary for help in making a list of as many additional compound words as he can.

Write the correct word under each picture. Put the two words together to make a new word.

Words to use:

pan	horse	hand	fly	shoe
bug	cup	tooth	board	brush
bag	lady	cake	butter	

 +  =

_____ + _____ = _____

+ =

_____ + _____ = _____

 +  =

_____ + _____ = _____

 + =

_____ + _____ = _____

 + 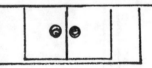 =

_____ + _____ = _____

 + =

_____ + _____ = _____

 +  =

_____ + _____ = _____

NOW

Write the correct word under each picture. Put the two words together to make a new word.

 + =

_____ _____ _____

 + =

_____ _____ _____

 + =

_____ _____ _____

 +  =

_____ _____ _____

 + =

_____ _____ _____

 +  =

_____ _____ _____

 + =

_____ _____ _____

 + = =

_____ _____ _____

WOW

191

butter	Compound words are made of two smaller words. See how many new words you can make by putting the words on this page together.	sales
man		cup
shoe		berry
cake		bug
melon		room
black	for example:	pan
mush	butter fly	board
bed	1._____	boy
horse	2._____	cow
water	3._____	mail
fly	4._____	sand
milk	5._____	box
school	6._____	fall
straw	7._____	rain
lady	8._____	fire
paper	9._____	house
store	10._____	horn
class	11._____	mate
news	12._____	back
	13._____	

 Write a sentence using each compound word you made. (For extra help, use a dictionary.)

Alphabet Annie

CENTRAL PURPOSE:

Alphabetizing

CENTER OBJECTIVES:

After completing this center the student should be able to:

(1)   arrange letters in alphabetical order.
(2)   order words alphabetically.
(3)   use alphabetical order to arrange words in sentences.

PROCEDURE:

1.   Place activity sheets, pencils, crayons, glue, and poster board in the center.

2.   Verbally introduce the center activities in a "fun" manner.

3.   Arrange time for guidance and continuing evaluation.

4.   Make provision for the student to glue completed activity sheets on poster board to make an attractive poster to be displayed in the classroom.

Alphabet Annie is having a terrible time trying to learn to use her dictionary. One of her problems is that she has never learned to put words in alphabetical order. Her teacher designed this center to help her. See if you can complete all the activities correctly so that you will not find yourself in the same predicament.

Begin by arranging the letters in Alphabet Annie's soup bowl in alphabetical order.

A ___ ___ ___ ___ ___ ___ ___ ___ ___ ___

___ ___ ___ ___ ___ ___ ___ ___ ___

___ ___ ___ ___ ___ ___ ___ ___ ___

___ Z ___

196

Find these words in the puzzle and circle them.

a	is	my	owe
an	mat	net	say
at	me	news	so
ate	men	no	yes

a	n	o	i
n	e	w	s
a	t	e	a
m	e	m	y
e	s	a	e
n	o	t	s

Extra Stuff → Put all the words you found in the puzzle in alphabetical order.

NOW

Alphabetize the words in each box. Write the words in alphabetical order in the blank spaces to make a sentence.

dogs	angry	growl
_____	_____	_____

high	birds	fly
_____	_____	_____

munching	elephants	peanuts	love
_____	_____	_____	_____

a	the	cow	fell	careless	in	water
___	___	___	___	___	___	___

 Extra Stuff) Capitalize and punctuate each sentence.

 WOW

Alphabetize the words in each box. Write the words in alphabetical order in the blank spaces to make a sentence.

good   very   swinger   a   well   swings

___ ___ _____ ___ ____ _____

me   smile   cartoons   make

___ ___ ____ _____

reading   sad   Tom   after   weeps   stories

_____ ___ ____ _____ _____ _____

begged   Al   wash   Bob   weekly   to

___ __ ____ _____ ____ _____

 Extra Stuff Capitalize and punctuate each sentence.

 WOW

1. Alphabetize the words in each box.
2. Write the words in alphabetical order in the blank spaces to make a sentence.
3. Draw a line from the sentence to the picture that best describes it.

canoes   can   crocodiles   crazy   carry

___   ___   ___   ___   ___

watching   win   wonderful   was   Willy

___   ___   ___   ___   ___

her   fed   Dora   kangaroo   olives   daffy
oily   jumping

___   ___   ___   ___   ___   ___

___   ___   ___

drawings   Debbie   drab   dear   does

___   ___   ___   ___   ___

happy   has   humor   Harry   horrible
handsome

___   ___   ___   ___   ___   ___

___

sick   saved   sailors   sinking   sailing
survivors   seven

___   ___   ___   ___   ___

___   ___   ___

 Capitalize and punctuate each sentence.

Make up your own "alphabetical" sentences.

Computer Match

CENTRAL PURPOSE:

Organizing Information

CENTER OBJECTIVES:

After completing this center the student should be able to:

(1)   gather specific information.
(2)   record information gained.
(3)   compute data in a meaningful sense.

PROCEDURE:

1.   Place activity sheets, pencils, and scratch paper in the center.

2.   Verbally introduce the center and provide motivation for its completion by leading a discussion on how gathering and categorizing information can make daily life easier and more interesting.

3.   Arrange for a free traffic flow and flexibility in scheduling to allow students to work together to complete the activities.

4.   Make provision for ongoing evaluation and give as much immediate feedback as possible.

5.   Ask the student to organize the completed activities to take home to share with family members.

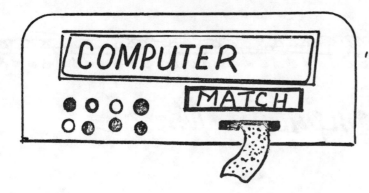

" Information Interviewing "

Interview friends with this "Computer Questionnaire".
Keep a record of the answers and match the people who have the most in common.

ACTIVITY MATCH UP COMPUTER QUESTIONNAIRE

Procedure:

1.   Write in the names of the people interviewed.

2.   Ask each person if he likes to do each activity listed.
      (For example: "Do you like to go to the movies?")

3.   If the answer is "yes", put a check in the correct box.

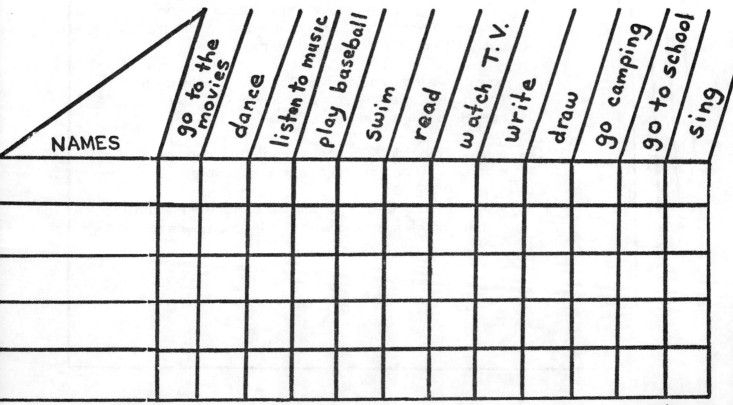

NAMES	go to the movies	dance	listen to music	play baseball	swim	read	watch T.V.	write	draw	go camping	go to school	sing

NOW

COMPATIBLE COMPANIONS
÷

Answer these questions about yourself:

(1) What is the color of your eyes?   (1) _____

(2) What is the color of your hair?   (2) _____

(3) What is the month of your birthday?   (3) _____

(4) Where were you born?   (4) _____

(5) What letter does your first name
    start with?   (5) _____

(6) What is your favorite food?   (6) _____

(7) What is your least favorite food?   (7) _____

(8) What is your favorite color?   (8) _____

(9) What is your favorite song?   (9) _____

(10) What is your favorite school
     subject?   (10) _____

(11) What is your favorite sport?   (11) _____

(12) What is your favorite television
     show?   (12) _____

Write the answers to your questions in the numbered spaces on the
Computer Sheet for Compatible Companions.

Example: If your answer to #1 is brown, you will write "brown" in space #1:

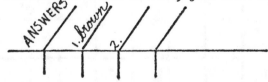

Interview your friends, asking them the same questions you answered
about yourself. If their answers match yours, put a check in the
correct box beside their names.

Count the checks to see which friend has the most in common with you.

WOW

COMPUTER SHEET

for

COMPATIBLE COMPANIONS

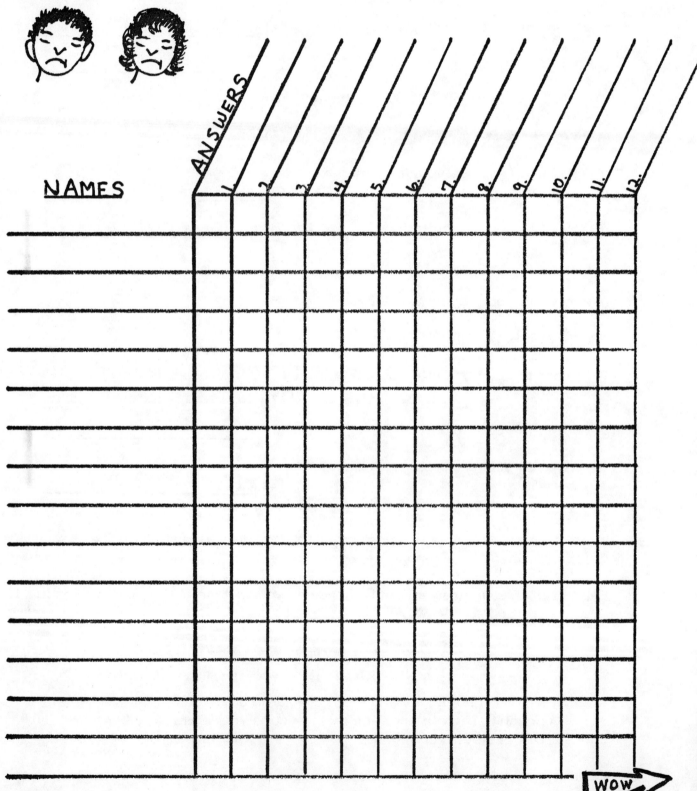

NAMES

ANSWERS

1. 2. 3. 4. 5. 6. 7. 8. 9. 10. 11. 12.

WOW

Use a black felt tip marker to draw a portrait of your most compatible companion.

Write your own interview questions. Suggested topics for questions are: sports, television, clothes, music, food, hobbies, home responsibilities, future plans, etc. Record questions and data on the interview computer form below.

1. _____

2. _____

3. _____

4. _____

5. _____

6. _____

7. _____

. . . .

INTERVIEW COMPUTER FORM

NAMES

	1.	2.	3.	4.	5.	6.	7.

POW

Concrete Charlie's Correction Corner

CENTRAL PURPOSE:

Punctuation and Word Usage

CENTER OBJECTIVES:

After completing this center the student should be able to:

(1)   use punctuation marks correctly.
(2)   use contractions and abbreviations.
(3)   find and correct mistakes in written materials.

PROCEDURE:

1.   Make a large paper cutout of Concrete Charlie and place it on a bulletin board near the center. Around Charlie's head place question marks, periods, etc. cut from construction paper. Place activity sheets, reference books, and pencils in the center.

2.   Explain each of the center activities and encourage the student to use one of the reference books for help if needed.

3.   Provide time for evaluation of each completed activity and give immediate feedback.

4.   Ask the student to select one completed activity sheet that he feels is representative of his best work and add it to the bulletin board display.

Charlie spells out everything, even punctuation marks. Read this letter
that he wrote to Mary. Rewrite the letter correctly at the bottom of the page.

Wed period comma Sept period eight

Dear Mary comma new paragraph I apostrophe m going

to have a party on Friday comma September ten at

four o apostrophe clock period Will you be able to

come question mark new paragraph I talked to Jim and

he said comma quotation marks I would love to come

to the party exclamation point quotation marks new

paragraph I think that a lot of people will be there

period I hope that you will be there too exclamation

point new paragraph I apostrophe ll be anxious to hear

your reply period

Sincerely comma

Charlie

Rewrite this story. To save time and space use these abbreviations and contractions in place of the underlined words:

bldg.	25	doz.	Mrs.	eve.	Mass.	Blvd.
			Mr.	didn't	Calif.	morn.
			Jr.	sta.	St.	Feb.
			Dr.	couldn't	Ave.	wouldn't
			apt.	Miss	Jan.	Wed.
				Mon.		

Charlie Smith, Junior had a doctor's appointment on Monday, January twenty-fifth. The doctor's office was in an office building on the corner of Mississippi Street and California Drive.

Charlie's neighbor, Mister Smith, offered to drive him in his car from their apartment building on Massachusetts Boulevard to the doctor's office. Unfortunately Mister Smith's car did not start.

Charlie went to the bus station, but the bus did not stop. He called a dozen taxis, but they could not come.

It was so late that he called the doctor's telephone number to talk to the nurse, Mistress Lee. He told her he would not be able to come to the office that morning for his appointment and asked if he could make another one for the first Wednesday evening in February.

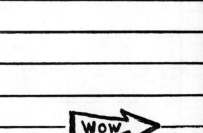

209

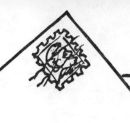

15 away place
birmingham : Michigan
May 10,19

Sound Record Company
main Stree
Detroit, Michigan

Dear sir

    I would like to apply for the job
you advertised in the skool newspaper.

    i am a good worker? I can work
in the afternoon and all day on
saturday.

    I want to learn more about the
job. please right to me at the above
Address.

    "Thank you."

        Sincerely...

        Charlie

Find and circle
17 errors
Charlie made in
this letter.
Correct the
mistakes and
rewrite the
letter below.

POW

Direction Detection

CENTRAL PURPOSE:

Following Directions

CENTER OBJECTIVES:

After completing this center the student should be able to:

(1) follow simple written directions.
(2) follow directions dependent on picture interpretation.
(3) find answers to puzzles by following directions.

PROCEDURE:

1. Arrange the center attractively with a bulletin board or other display area in the background. Place activity sheets, black and blue felt tip markers, and blue, red, yellow, green, black, brown, pink, and orange colored chalk in the center, along with scissors and glue. Label the display area "Hidden Numbers".

2. Discuss the importance of learning to follow directions (perhaps telling a funny story about someone who did not know how to follow directions). Introduce the center activities in detail to enable the student to work as independently as possible.

3. Instruct the student to find and color the hidden numbers as directed on the activity sheet and to cut out the finished design to add collage fashion to the bulletin board display.

4. Provide ongoing guidance and evaluation to encourage completion of the other activities.

Draw a circle around the numbers you find.

Color the 1 blue.

Color the 2 red.

Color the 3 yellow.

Color the 4 green.

Color the 5 black.

Color the 6 red.

Color the 7 brown.

Color the 8 pink.

Color the 9 orange.

1.   Color the dress of the girl wearing a big hat red.

2.   Color the book the short girl is carrying blue.

3.   Color the tall boy's sweater red.

4.   Color the short boy's shirt yellow.

5.   Color the tall girl's hat red and blue.

6.   Color the short boy's hat green and yellow.

Extra Stuff

Ask your friend questions about the picture. Be sure his answers are complete sentences.

Suggested questions:

1. What does the short girl have?
2. Who has a yellow shirt?
3. Who has a red dress?
4. Who is wearing a hat?
5. Who is not wearing a hat?

The pirates their treasure
    did take
To a hiding place
    by the lake.
These directions they left
    to help you
Search for the clue.

1. Cross out the first circle.

2. Circle the largest circle.

3. Put an X on the smallest square.

4. Circle the middle square

5. Underline the last triangle.

6. Circle the second triangle.

7. Color in the third oval.

8. Circle the next to last oval.

9. Write the letter of shape circled.

If you followed the directions the pirates gave,
you found their hiding place to be a _____. WOW

Follow the directions given below to reach your "mystery" destination.

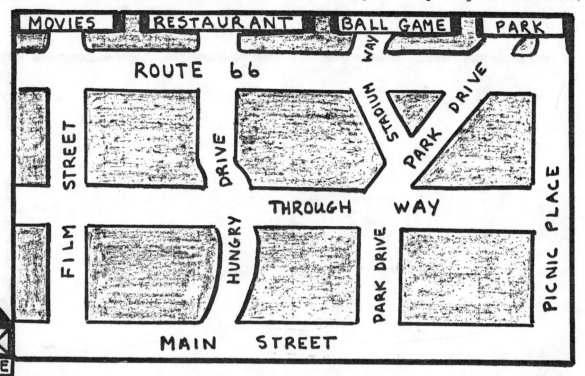

MYSTERY CAR RIDE #1

1. Start at <u>Home</u>.

2. Drive straight on Main Street.

3. Drive to Hungry Drive and turn left.

4. Drive to Through Way and turn right.

5. Drive to Picnic Place and turn right.

6. Drive to Main Street and turn right.

7. Drive to Film Street and turn right.

8. Drive straight on Film Street to your destination.

You are at the _____.
What will you do there?

MYSTERY CAR RIDE #2

1. Start at <u>Home</u>.

2. Drive north on Film Street to Route 66.

3. Drive east on Route 66.

4. Drive south on Hungry Drive.

5. Drive east on Through Way.

6. Drive northeast on Park Drive.

7. Drive northwest on Stadium Way.

8. Drive west on Route 66.

9. Drive north on Hungry Drive to your destination.

You are at the _____.
What will you do there?

215

Make up your own set of mystery directions and ask a friend to follow them.

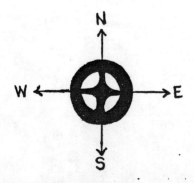
HOME

Draw a picture to make the directions more interesting and to give clues to solving the mystery.

Direct~O~Gram

CENTRAL PURPOSE:

Following Directions

CENTER OBJECTIVES:

After completing this center the student should be able to:

(1)   follow oral directions.
(2)   read directions orally.
(3)   follow written directions.

PROCEDURE:

1.   Place activity sheets, rulers, and pencils in the center.

2.   Verbally introduce the center.

3.   Arrange for two students to work together to complete center activities and provide guidance and ongoing evaluation as needed.

4.   Make provision for filing or displaying completed activities.

Give a friend the "Direct-o-gram", a pencil, and a ruler. Read these directions and ask him to follow them to discover the secret design.

1. Draw a line from G-4 to A-4.
2. Draw a line from D-1 to D-7.
3. Draw a line from G-4 to E-3.
4. Draw a line from E-3 to D-1.
5. Draw a line from D-1 to C-3.
6. Draw a line from C-3 to A-4.

7. Draw a line from A-4 to C-5.
8. Draw a line from C-5 to D-7.
9. Draw a line from D-7 to E-5.
10. Draw a line from E-5 to G-4.
11. Draw a line from E-3 to C-5.
12. Draw a line from C-3 to E-5.

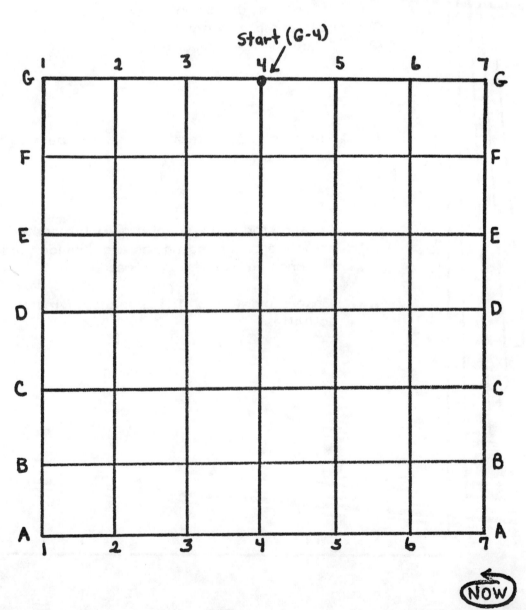

218

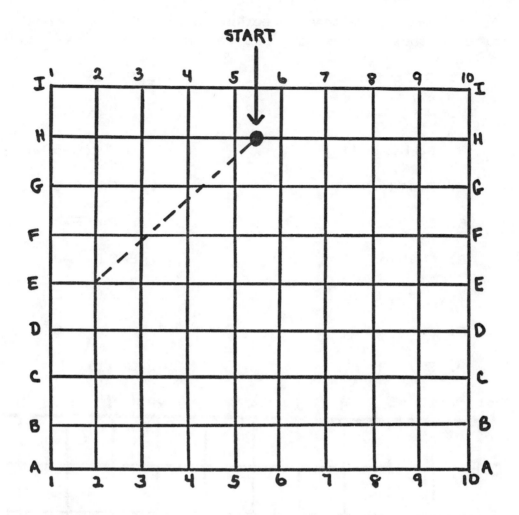

Read the directions and follow them to discover the secret design.

1. Draw a line from START to point E-2 (as shown on the dotted line).
2. Draw a line from START to point E-9.

Draw lines between these points:

3. E-2 to B-2
4. B-2 to B-9
5. B-9 to E-9
6. E-2 to E-9
7. C-3 to C-4
8. C-4 to D-4
9. D-4 to D-3
10. D-3 to C-3
11. B-5 to D-5
12. D-5 to D-6

13. D-6 to B-6
14. C-7 to C-8
15. C-8 to D-8
16. D-8 to D-7
17. D-7 to C-7

18. Draw a circle in the lower right-hand corner of square (C-D-5-6).

Ask a friend to read these directions to you. Follow the oral directions to reveal the secret design. Draw a line between these points:

1. G–2 to I–5
2. I–5 to I–11
3. I–11 to D–11
4. D–11 to D–10
5. D–10 to G–10
6. G–10 to F–8
7. F–8 to B–8
8. B–8 to B–7
9. B–7 to F–7

10. F–7 to F–3
11. F–6 to D–6
12. D–6 to D–5
13. D–5 to F–5
14. F–3 to B–3
15. B–3 to B–2
16. B–2 to G–2
17. G–2 to G–8
18. G–8 to I–11

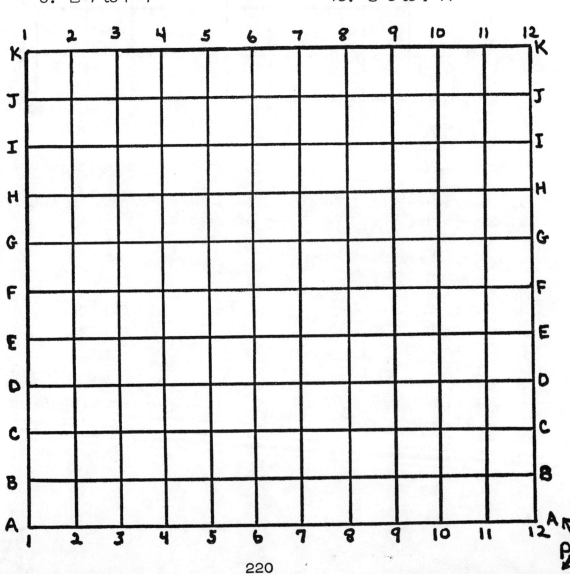

If True, Do

CENTRAL PURPOSE:

Decision Making

CENTER OBJECTIVES:

After completing this center the student should be able to:

(1) follow directions on the basis of decision making.
(2) use written clues to arrive at a logical conclusion.
(3) use creative resources to develop a puzzle.

PROCEDURE:

1. Place activity sheets, pencils, crayons, glue, scissors, and tagboard in the center.

2. Verbally introduce the center and discuss each puzzle in enough detail to allow the student to work independently.

3. Arrange to give ongoing guidance as the activity sheets are being completed.

4. Make provision for the student to cut each completed puzzle out and glue it to a tagboard backing to form a "set" of puzzle cards to be shared with friends or family.

To solve the puzzle and find the hidden word, read the sentences below. If the statement is <u>true,</u> color the numbered puzzle spaces as directed.

5	2	7	6	4	7
					2
9	9 1	5	3	9	5
	3 6				8
7	8	4	2	4	1

If you see with your eyes, color the #1 spaces.

If you talk with your ears, color the #2 spaces.

If you walk on your lips, color the #3 spaces.

If you wiggle your toes, color the #4 spaces.

If you touch with your fingers, color the #5 spaces.

If you chew with your hands, color the #6 spaces.

If you smell with your nose, color the #7 spaces.

If your mouth is above your nose, color the #8 spaces.

If you bend at the waist, color the #9 spaces.

222

To solve the puzzle and find the hidden word, read the sentences below. If the statement is _true_, color the numbered puzzle spaces as directed.

```
| 11          7 |8| 10        2 |4| 1 | 13 |
| 4      14     |5| 6 | 16 | 15 |12|14|16| 7 |
|12   1      3  | 13 | 8 | 11 |8|17| 5 | 15 |
| 9        6    |5|    2    |3|  9  13| 10 |
                                          1
```

If cows give milk, color the #1 spaces.

If whales swim, color the #2 spaces.

If birds have scales, color the #3 spaces.

If roosters lay eggs, color the #4 spaces.

If lions have stripes, color the #5 spaces.

If camels have humps, color the #6 spaces.

If pigs "oink", color the #7 spaces.

If snakes are mammals, color the #8 spaces.

If squirrels eat nuts, color the #9 spaces.

If elephants have trunks, color the #10 spaces.

If a zebra has stripes, color the #11 spaces.

If chickens "quack", color the #12 spaces.

If spiders spin webs, color the #13 spaces.

If cats have fur, color the #14 spaces.

If an ant is an insect, color the #15 spaces.

If worms have feet, color the #16 spaces.

If eagles have feathers, color the #17 spaces.

223

To solve the puzzle and find the hidden word, read the sentences below.
If the statement is <u>true</u>, color the numbered puzzle spaces as directed.

2\1	5 /15 /8	13	11	14 /1	3	9	4
20	17 \3 /4 / 13	2	6	3 /16	20	17	2
2	18 6 16	12	19	22/1 / 22	8	5	16	10
21	9	5	23	22	21	23	14	7	15
3	7	13\21	16	6	19	13	11	1

If grass is green, color the #1 spaces.
If colors can be heard, color the #2 spaces.
If nouns are action words, color the #3 spaces.
If cars have wheels, color the #4 spaces.
If fish live in the air, color the #5 spaces.
If houses have rooms, color the #6 spaces.
If ice melts, color the #7 spaces.
If a bicycle has three wheels, color the #8 spaces.
If a tricycle has three wheels, color the #9 spaces.
If the letter "U" is a vowel, color the #10 spaces.
If a guitar is an instrument, color the #11 spaces.
If a baseball is a plant, color the #12 spaces.
If fire is cold, color the #13 spaces.
If hair grows, color the #14 spaces.
If scissors cut, color the #15 spaces.
If machines are alive, color the #16 spaces.
If the earth is a planet, color the #17 spaces.
If the sun is a star, color the #18 spaces.
If cities have streets, color the #19 spaces.
If rocks are food, color the #20 spaces.
If long means the same as short, color the #21 spaces.
If a library has books, color the #22 spaces.
If telephones answer, color the #23 spaces.

224

To solve the puzzle and find the hidden country, read the sentences below. If the statement is <u>true</u>, color the numbered puzzle spaces as directed.

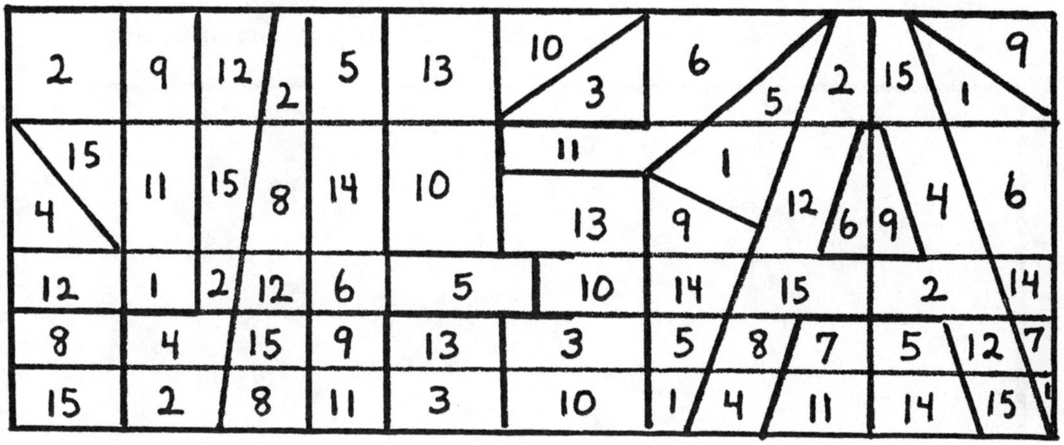

2	9	12	2	5	13	10	3	6	5	2	15	1	9

(puzzle grid with numbered spaces)

Row values as drawn:
2, 9, 12, 2, 5, 13, 10, 3, 6, 5, 2, 15, 1, 9
15, 4, 11, 15, 8, 14, 10, 11, 13, 1, 9, 12, 6, 9, 4, 6
12, 1, 2, 12, 6, 5, 10, 14, 15, 2, 14
8, 4, 15, 9, 13, 3, 5, 8, 7, 5, 12, 7
15, 2, 8, 11, 3, 10, 1, 4, 11, 14, 15

If Mississippi is an ocean, color the #1 spaces blue.

If Tennessee is a state, color the #2 spaces red.

If Hawaii is a state, color the #3 spaces blue.

If Mexico is a country, color the #4 spaces red.

If Michigan is a country, color the #5 spaces red.

If Florida is a river, color the #6 spaces blue.

If Kentucky is in South America, color the #7 spaces red.

If Canada is a country, color the #8 spaces red.

If Washington, D. C. is the capital of Canada, color the #9 spaces blue.

If Washington is a state, color the #10 spaces blue.

If Ohio is an island, color the #11 spaces blue.

If New York is a city, color the #12 spaces red.

If California borders an ocean, color the #13 spaces blue.

If England is a continent, color the #14 spaces red.

If Australia is an island, color the #15 spaces red.

225

Design your own puzzle. Write directions for finding the hidden word.
Ask a friend to solve the puzzle.

Use one of the following topics:

A sport   School
Television programs   Your own city or town
Holidays   Famous Americans

Memory Box

CENTRAL PURPOSE:

Descriptive Recall

CENTER OBJECTIVES:

After completing this center the student should be able to:

(1)   arrange words in sequence according to descriptive verbal instructions.
(2)   sequentially order numbers for recall discussion.
(3)   use recall skills to break a letter–number code.

PROCEDURE:

1.   Place activity sheets, scissors, pencils, and additional writing paper in the center.

2.   Provide motivation for the center by playing some simple memory games or by role-playing funny situations which may occur because of lack of memory.

3.   Introduce the center in as much detail as necessary and arrange for students to work in pairs to complete activities.

4.   Provide guidance and ongoing evaluation.

5.   Arrange for students to keep word and number cards at their desks for future use and to share the decoded message sheets in a "fun" group setting.

Cut the picture cards apart.

Say a word sequence to a friend (for example: sun–house–star). Ask him to find the correct picture cards and place them in the same order.

Suggested Sequences:

Level I	Level II	Level III
mushroom–gift–ball	star–ball–sun–bee	cup–sun–bee–house–moon

1	4	7
2	5	8
3	6	9

Cut the cards apart.

Say a number sequence to a friend (for example: 7 – 3 – 6). Ask him to find the correct number cards and place them in the same order.

Suggested Sequences:

Level I	Level II	Level III	Level IV
8 – 6	6 – 8 – 2 – 5	5 – 1 – 9 – 3 – 7	4 – 6 – 1 – 7 – 3 – 2
4 – 2 – 7	3 – 1 – 7 – 4	2 – 9 – 8 – 6 – 4	5 – 2 – 8 – 7 – 9 – 1
6 – 1 – 5	9 – 6 – 2 – 7	3 – 6 – 9 – 8 – 1	8 – 9 – 4 – 1 – 6 – 5

Give a friend a copy of this letter–number code.

A	B	C	D	E	F	G	H	I	J	K	L	M
1	2	3	4	5	6	7	8	9	10	11	12	13
N	O	P	Q	R	S	T	U	V	W	X	Y	Z
14	15	16	17	18	19	20	21	22	23	24	25	26

Spell the words given below in numbers. Ask your friend to listen carefully and to "decode" the word. Ask him to "act out" the decoded message.

Action Code	Answer
18 · 21 · 14	r·u·n
19 · 9 · 20	
8 · 15 · 16	
3 · 18 · 25	
6 · 1 · 12 · 12	
25 · 5 · 12 · 12	
23 · 1 · 12 · 11	
10 · 21 · 13 · 16	
19 · 11 · 9 · 16	
12 · 1 · 21 · 7 · 8	
19 · 13 · 9 · 12 · 5	
6 · 18 · 15 · 23 · 14	
20 · 9 · 16 · 20 · 15 · 5	

Direction	Code	Answer
Touch your	20·15·5·19	t·o·e·s
Wiggle your	14·15·19·5	
Blink your	5·25·5·19	
Stomp your	6·15·15·20	
Scratch your	2·1·3·11	
Sit on your	3·8·1·9·18	
Clap your	8·1·14·4·19	
Open your	13·15·21·20·8	
Bend your	5·12·2·15·23	
Snap your	6·9·14·7·5·18·19	

Extra Stuff → Use the number code to "spell" the names of your classmates. POW

Reference Referral

CENTRAL PURPOSE:

Using Reference Materials

CENTER OBJECTIVES:

After completing this center the student should be able to:

(1) use the telephone directory to gain information.
(2) make meaningful use of the dictionary.
(3) select appropriate reference materials to secure specific information.

PROCEDURE:

1. Place activity sheets, pencils, telephone directory, dictionary, newspapers, encyclopedias, catalogs, thesaurus, cookbook, etiquette books and drivers' manual in the center.

2. Introduce the center and extend the discussion to focus on instruction for each activity.

3. Arrange for students to work in pairs to complete activities and provide guidance and ongoing evaluation as needed.

4. Make provision for filing completed activities for later referral.

Find these words in the puzzle and circle them:

```
m e c h a n i c e
a c r w p q d a l
i z t a i l o r e
d m a i l m a n c
d o c t o r x y t
l u v e t a c f r
a f o r e o l a i
w t e a c h e r c
y b a r b e r m i
e i n g e r k e a
r o w e l d e r n
s e c r e t a r y
```

secretary
welder
clerk
mechanic
lawyer
waiter
farmer
electrician
doctor
maid
tailor
mailman
teacher
barber
pilot

Extra Stuff → List the puzzle words in alphabetical order. Look them up in the dictionary and define each occupation.

For example: barber - a person whose business is cutting and styling hair.

Write the names of ten friends in alphabetical order. Use the telephone book to find their addresses and telephone numbers. Record the information below.

NAME	ADDRESS AND TELEPHONE NUMBER

PERSONAL DIRECTORY by

Extra stuff) Find out your friends birthdays. Write the special date under each name.

WOW

A dictionary is a useful book of and about words. It will tell you what a word means, how to pronounce it, how to use it in a sentence, and how it is spelled.

It is easy to find a word in the dictionary. All the words are listed in alphabetical order. Two guide words are at the top of each page. The word on the left tells the first word to be found on that page. The word on the right tells the last word on the page.

There are games that can be played with the dictionary. One game to play with a friend is called the "Word Race". In this game a word is given and the players see who can find it in the dictionary first. Another game to play is the "Longest Word". Each player opens his dictionary to a page and finds the longest word on the page. Each letter in the word is worth one point. The person with the most points wins the game.

Using the information above, complete the details in this outline.

REFERENCE BOOKS

I. The Dictionary
   A. Uses of the dictionary

      1. _____
      2. _____
      3. _____
      4. _____

   B. Finding words in the dictionary

      1. _____
      2. _____
        a. _____
        b. _____

   C. Dictionary games to play

      1. _____
      2. _____

Outlining Steps

Extra Stuff: Write a report on another reference book. Outline your information as Roman Numeral II.

WOW

234

Atlas   Thesaurus
Dictionary   Encyclopedia
Newspaper   Telephone Directory
Cookbook   Etiquette Book
Store Catalog   Drivers' Manual

Which of the reference sources above would you use to find information about the following topics?

1. World Maps _____

2. The price of a gift _____

3. A person's address _____

4. How to set a table _____

5. The meaning of a word _____

6. Speed limits _____

7. The history of a country _____

8. The pronunciation of a word _____

9. Synonyms and antonyms _____

10. Recipes _____

11. Current events _____

12. Biographies of famous people _____

13. Correct ways to write a letter _____

14. Area Codes _____

Extra Stuff Make a list of five things you can find in each reference source used on this page.

Use the reference sources to find answers to these questions.

1. What is a kazoo? _____

_____

2. What is the birth date of George Washington? _____

_____

3. How many eggs are in a sponge cake? _____

_____

4. What should you wear to an afternoon wedding? _____

_____

5. What is the weather forecast for today? _____

_____

6. What is the area code for Chicago, Illinois? _____

_____

7. What five words are synonymous with jump? _____

_____

8. What states border Idaho? _____

_____

9. What is the longest river in the world and where is it?

_____

10. What is the speed limit for trucks on interstate highways?

_____

Extra Stuff — Use reference books to make up your own trivia questions. Ask a friend to find their answers.

Schedule Schemers

CENTRAL PURPOSE:

Making Schedules

CENTER OBJECTIVES:

After completing this center the student should be able to:

(1)   plan a personal time schedule.
(2)   plan a schedule within the framework of given
      time blocks.
(3)   budget time and develop a schedule for completion
      of a variety of activities.

PROCEDURE:

1.   Place activity sheets, pencils, drawing paper, and
     tempera paint in the center.

2.   Verbally introduce the center.

3.   Instruct the student to select two or three friends
     with which to discuss the projected schedules.
     This verbal interaction may be motivational and
     may also serve to clarify developing concepts.

4.   Arrange conference time for discussion and
     evaluation of the completed activities and provide
     reinforcement as needed.

5.   Encourage the student to use the art materials
     to illustrate a typical day according to one of the
     schedules developed.

Learn to make good use of your time by planning and carrying out schedules. A good place to begin is by planning for your "free time". Plan a schedule for this week-end.

	MORNING	AFTERNOON
FRIDAY	In School	
SATURDAY		
SUNDAY		

NOW

Fill in a schedule you would like for summer camp. Mark your first, second, and third choices in each category. Try to balance your schedule with one class from each group and as many of your first choices as possible.

CAMP SCHEDULE

Choices			Class	Time	
1st	2nd	3rd			
			Art and Painting	9:00–10:00 a.m.	Arts and Crafts
			Music	10:00–11:00 a.m.	
			Sewing	1:00– 2:00 p.m.	
			Woodworking	2:00– 3:00 p.m.	
			Driver Education	10:00–11:00 a.m.	Educational
			Cooking	11:00–12:00 a.m.	
			Typing	1:00– 2:00 p.m.	
			Bird Watching	2:00– 3:00 p.m.	
			Nature Study	3:00– 4:00 p.m.	
			Tennis	9:00–10:00 a.m.	Sports
			Gym	11:00–12:00 a.m.	
			Bowling	2:00– 3:00 p.m.	
			Swimming	3:00– 4:00 p.m.	
			Karate	3:00– 4:00 p.m.	

Time	Class
9:00 – 10:00 A.M.	
10:00 – 11:00 A.M.	
11:00 – 12:00 P.M.	
12:00 – 1:00 P.M.	
1:00 – 2:00 P.M.	
2:00 – 3:00 P.M.	
3:00 – 4:00 P.M.	

Extra Stuff ⟶ Make a camp schedule for a friend.

Make a schedule to help you remember all these instructions.

Your mother asked you to come home from the ball game at 1:00 p.m. because she has some errands for you to do. She told you that it is very important that you remember to do everything.

At 2:30 p.m. you are supposed to go to the library to return three books. By 3:00 p.m. you should be at the cleaners to pick up your father's suit. Your mother needed some glue and paper, so she asked you to plan to be at the drugstore by 3:30 p.m.

At 4:00 p.m. you are to go to the grocery store to buy bread, milk, and peanut butter. On your way home, at 5:00 p.m. you are to stop by Mrs. Smith's house to feed the dog and to pick up her mail.

Plan your schedule by making notes as follows:

Time	Where to go	What to do

Extra Stuff) List the five items Dave is supposed to buy..

_____   _____   _____

_____   _____

Shopping Center

CENTRAL PURPOSE:

Problem Solving

CENTER OBJECTIVES:

After completing this center the student should be able to:

(1)   relate analytically to a pictured situation.
(2)   use written clues to arrive at solutions to specific problems.
(3)   plan activities on the basis of information gained from following clues.

PROCEDURE:

1.   If possible arrange a field trip to a shopping center as motivation. If this is not possible, share a film strip, large flat picture, or library books featuring a shopping center theme.

2.   Place activity sheets and pencils in the center.

3.   Verbally introduce the center and discuss the shopping center directory in as much detail as necessary to give the student a clear understanding of its purpose and use.

4.   Extend the discussion to focus on separate activities to enable the student to work as independently as possible.

5.   Arrange conference time for discussion and evaluation of each completed activity and provide reinforcement as needed.

6.   Make provision for sharing completed activities in a group setting.

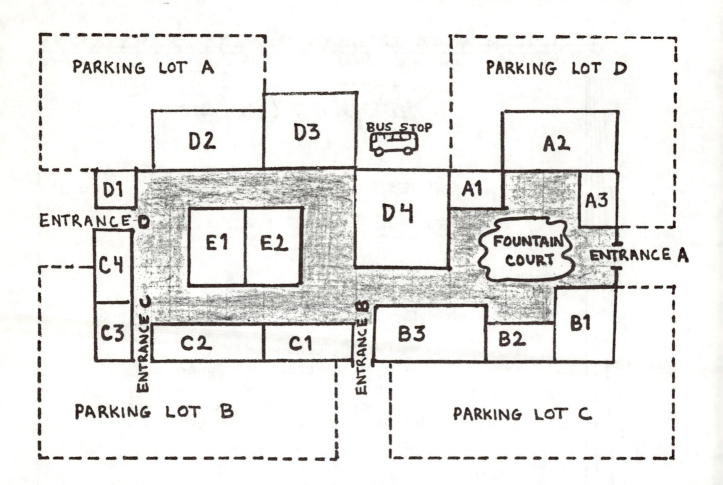

PARKING LOT A

D2

D3

BUS STOP

PARKING LOT D

A2

D1

A1

A3

ENTRANCE D

D4

FOUNTAIN COURT

ENTRANCE A

E1

E2

C4

ENTRANCE C

ENTRANCE B

C3

C2

C1

B3

B2

B1

PARKING LOT B

PARKING LOT C

SHOPPING CENTER DIRECTORY

Clothes

C-2	Kiddie Clothes Store
A-3	Mel's Men's Store
C-3	Jean's Casual Clothes
B-3	Young Lady Lovely

Food

D-4	Center Super Market
E-1	Don's Bakery

Furniture

A-2	Furniture Mart

Hobby, Pet & Leisure

C-1	Pal's Pet Store
E-2	Toys for All Ages
D-1	Book & Card Nook

Jewelry & Gifts

C-4	Jim's Gems & Gift Shop

Restaurant

A-1	Hap's Hamburger Heaven
D-3	The Fine Diner

Services

B-2	Beauty & Barber Salon
D-2	Center Bank & Trust
B-1	U. S. Post Office

NOW

Use the Shopping Center Directory to find the name of the store coded below. Write the store's name in the blank beside the picture that best describes it.

E-2 _____

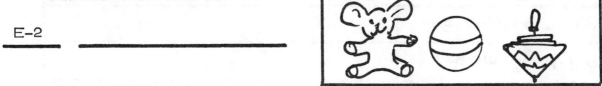

A-2 _____

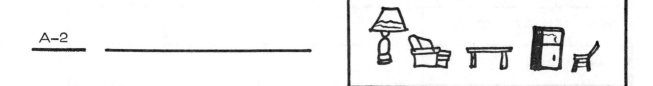

C-1 _____

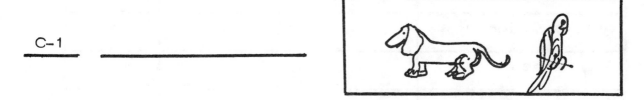

E-1 _____

A-1 _____

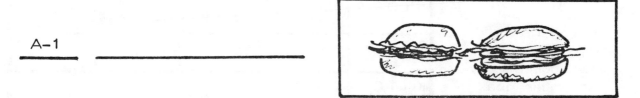

D-1 _____

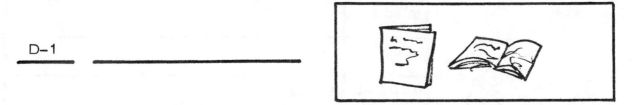

B-1 _____

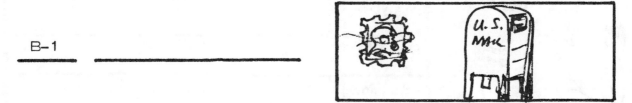

Use the Shopping Center Directory to find where you will go for each item on your shopping list. Record the name of the store and store code.

Things to Buy and Do	Where to Go (Name of Store)	Store Code
buy a birthday gift		
buy party clothes		
buy a birthday card		
buy ice cream		
buy grape juice		
have lunch		
go to bank for money		
buy shoes		
have hair cut		
buy a game to play at party		
buy birthday cake		

To save time and steps, schedule your shopping day. Remember, ice cream melts!

9:00 A.M.	Center Bank and Trust (D2)
9:30 A.M.	
10:00 A.M.	
10:30 A.M.	
11:00 A.M.	
11:30 A.M.	(Lunch)
12:30 P.M.	
1:00 P.M.	
1:30 P.M.	
2:00 P.M.	Beauty and Barber Salon (B2)
3:00 P.M.	

WOW

Use the shopping center directory to solve each of these parking problems.

Parking Problem #1

    You have to go to the <u>Furniture Mart</u> and the <u>Center Super Market</u>.

        Solution #1 –   You will park in Lot _____.
                             You will use Entrance _____.

Parking Problem #2

    You have to go to <u>Pal's Pet Shop</u> and <u>Jean's Casual Clothes</u>.

        Solution #2 –   You will park in Lot _____.
                             You will use Entrance _____.

Parking Problem #3

    You have to go to the <u>U. S. Post Office</u>, <u>Toys for All Ages</u>, and to <u>Fountain Court</u> to meet a friend.

        Solution #3 –   You will park in Lot _____.
                             You will use Entrance _____.

Parking Problem #4

    You have to go to <u>Jim's Gems and Gift Shop</u>, <u>The Fine Diner</u>, and <u>Young Lady Lovely</u>.

        Solution #4 –   You will park in Lot _____.
                             You will use Entrance _____.

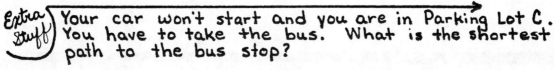

Extra Stuff Your car won't start and you are in Parking Lot C. You have to take the bus. What is the shortest path to the bus stop?

Design a shopping center of the future and include the kinds of stores you would like to shop in twenty years from now. Label all the stores and make a center directory.

SHOPPING CENTER DIRECTORY

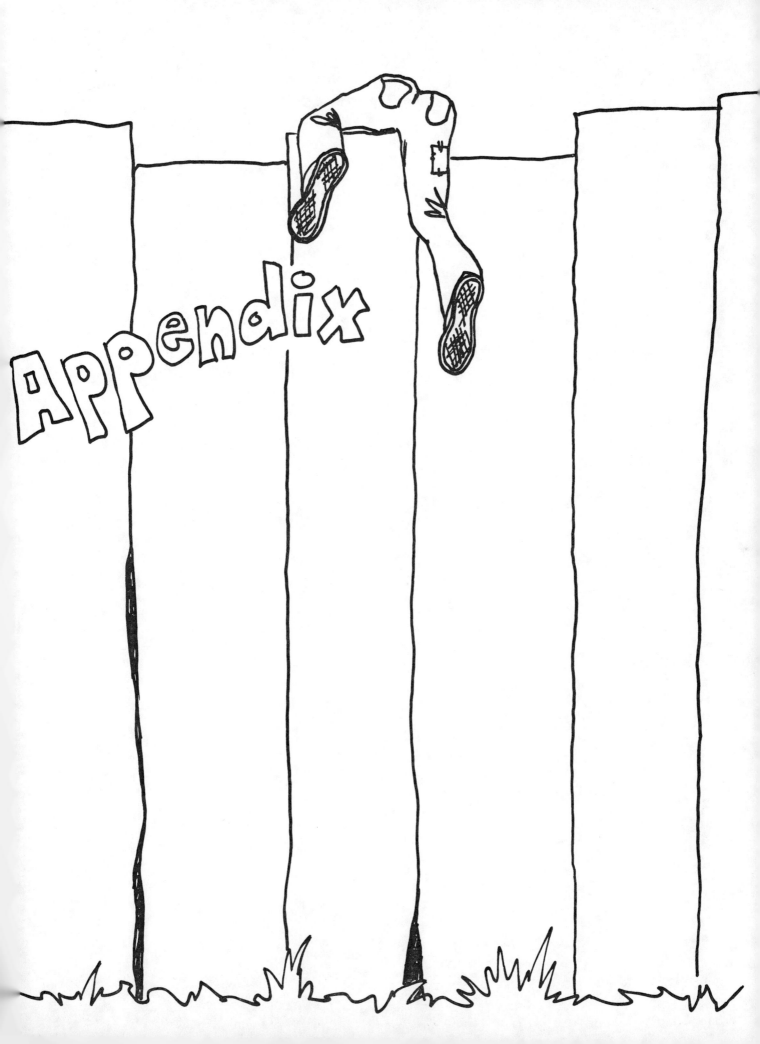

I SPY

Some students not yet ready to read or write for meaning may need more structured experiences designed to develop usual perception skills, visual motor skills, or visual and memory association skills. The following activity sheets have been developed for this purpose and should be used on an individual diagnostic-prescriptive basis.

Can you trace these lines?

→ means start

■ means stop

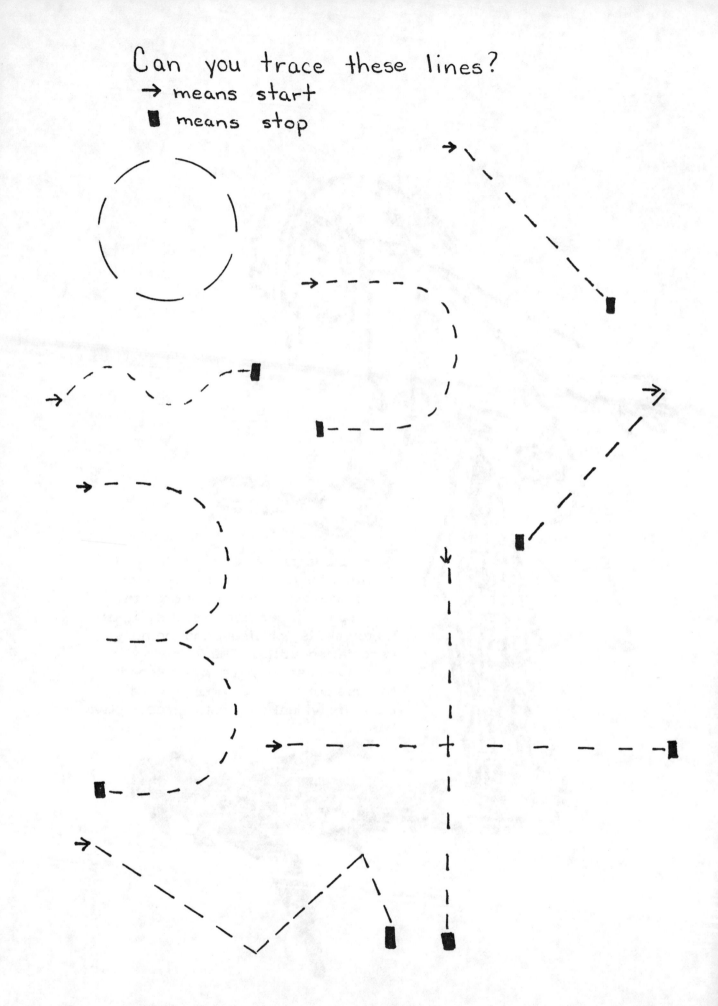

Trace and then copy these two drawings

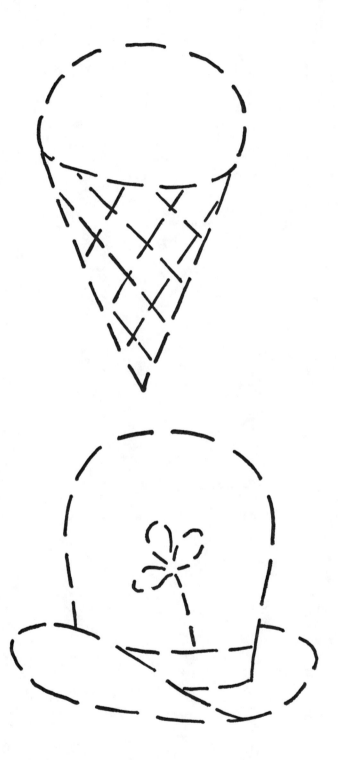

Copy the two designs.
Remember to shade them!

Copy these designs.

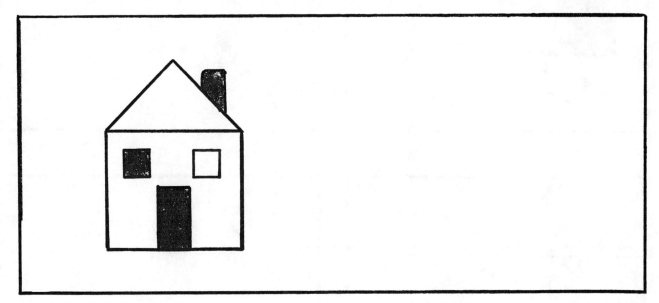

Copy these designs.

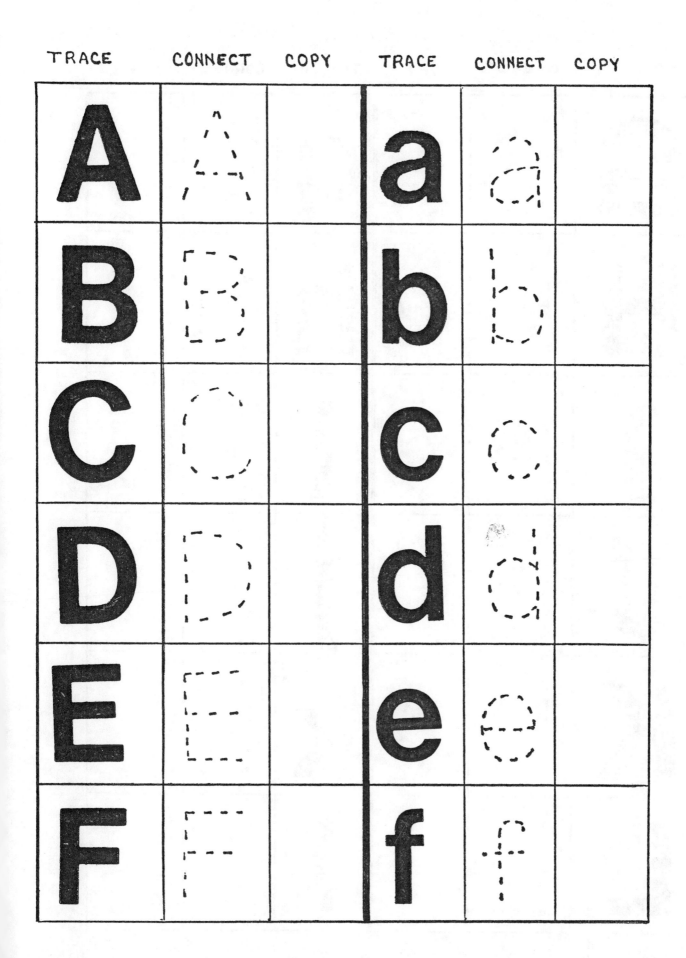

G	G		g	g	
H	H		h	h	
I	I		i	i	
J	J		j	j	
K	K		k	k	
L	L		l	l	

TRACE	CONNECT	COPY	TRACE	CONNECT	COPY
M	M		**m**	m	
N	N		**n**	n	
O	O		**o**	o	
P	P		**p**	p	
Q	Q		**q**	q	
R	R		**r**	r	

257

TRACE	CONNECT	COPY	TRACE	CONNECT	COPY
S	S		s	s	
T	T		t	t	
U	U		u	u	
V	V		V	V	
W	W		w	w	
X	X		x	x	

258

TRACE	CONNECT	COPY	TRACE	CONNECT	COPY
Y	Y		y	y	
Z	Z		z	z	

Trace	Copy	Trace	Copy	Trace	Copy
.		,		¢	
!		:		$	
?		"		&	

259

TRACE	CONNECT	COPY	TRACE	CONNECT	COPY
a	a		a	a	
B	B		b	b	
C	C		c	c	
D	D		d	d	
E	E		e	e	
F	F		f	f	

TRACE	CONNECT	COPY	TRACE	CONNECT	COPY
$\mathscr{G}$	$\mathscr{G}$		g	g	
$\mathscr{H}$	$\mathscr{H}$		h	h	
$\mathscr{I}$	$\mathscr{I}$		i	i	
$\mathscr{J}$	$\mathscr{J}$		j	j	
$\mathscr{K}$	$\mathscr{K}$		k	k	
$\mathscr{L}$	$\mathscr{L}$		l	l	

261

TRACE	CONNECT	COPY	TRACE	CONNECT	COPY
M	*M*		*m*	*m*	
N	*N*		*n*	*n*	
O	*O*		*o*	*o*	
P	*P*		*p*	*p*	
2	*2*		*q*	*q*	
R	*R*		*r*	*r*	

TRACE	CONNECT	COPY	TRACE	CONNECT	COPY
S	*S*		*s*	*s*	
T	*T*		*t*	*t*	
U	*U*		*u*	*u*	
V	*V*		*v*	*v*	
W	*W*		*w*	*w*	
X	*X*		*x*	*x*	

TRACE	CONNECT	COPY	TRACE	CONNECT	COPY
y	*y*		*y*	*y*	
z	*z*		*z*	*z*	

TRACE	COPY	TRACE	COPY	TRACE	COPY
ck		*ch*		*er*	
br		*bl*		*qu*	
wh		*ed*		*an*	

PUZZLE PLEASERS

A collection of crossword, word search, code, scramble word, and other puzzles to motivate and reinforce the development of basic language skills

COLOR WORD FIND

CROSSWORD CALENDAR

CROSSWORD OPPOSITES

DAFFY DEFINITIONS

DELIGHTFUL DAYS

FIND THE WORD

LETTER TREE

MONEY MIX-UP

NIMBLE NUMBERS

NUMBER WORD FIND

READY! GET SET! GO!!!!

RHYMING CROSSWORDS

SCRAMBLED SHOPPER

SECRET WORD

SENTENCE FORMULAS

SHAPE IN

WORDY PATH

WORD RING-AROUND

Find ten color words in the puzzle and circle them.

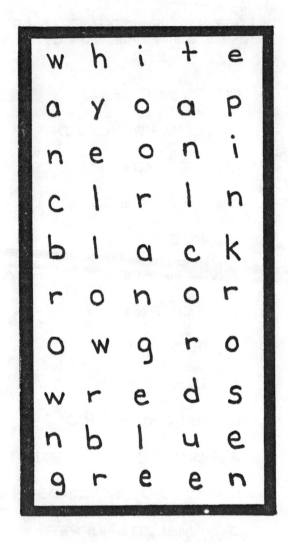

w h i t e
a y o a p
n e o n i
c l r l n
b l a c k
r o n o r
o w g r o
w r e d s
n b l u e
g r e e n

Extra Stuff) Write each of the color words you found in the puzzle. Use your crayons to illustrate each word.

Examples: <u>yellow</u>   <u>rose</u>

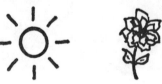

Match the month of the year to fit the descriptions listed.
Write the name of each month in the correct puzzle box.

Across:

1. The month that comes after May
3. The month that comes before October
5. _ _ _ _ _ showers bring May flowers
7. The hot month right after July
9. The first month of the year
11. The last month of the year

Down:

2. The month for Thanksgiving
4. The month for Valentine sharing
6. The flower month before June
8. A very windy month
10. The birthday month of the U. S. A.
12. The month for Halloween

Months

January   October
February   November
March   December
April
May
June
July
August
September

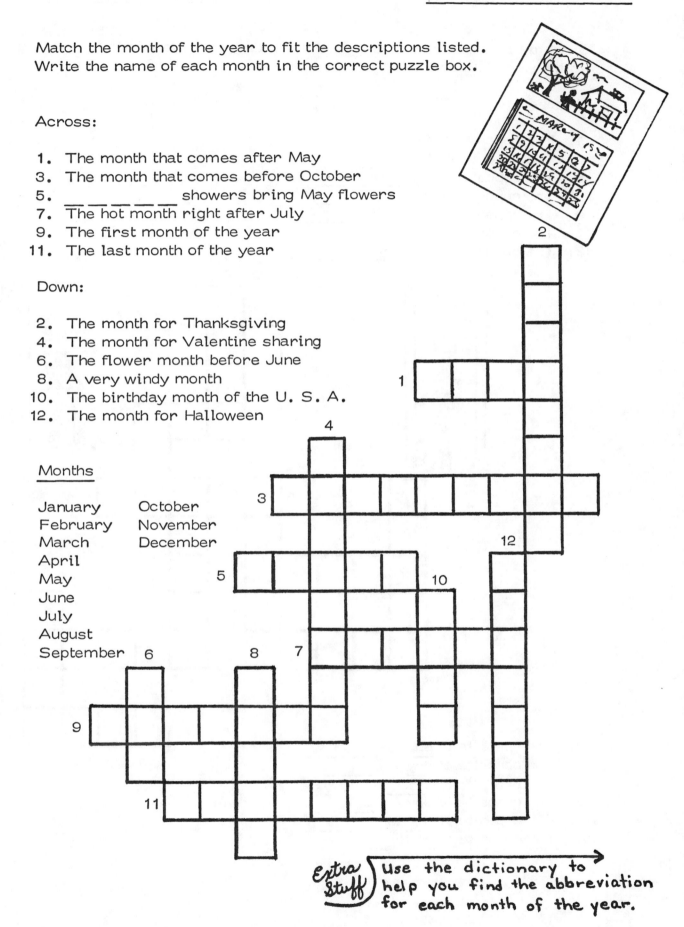

Extra Stuff Use the dictionary to help you find the abbreviation for each month of the year.

Work this crossword puzzle by using words that are opposite in meaning to the words underlined.

Across:

1. The opposite of <u>in</u> is _____.
3. The opposite of <u>high</u> is _____.
5. The opposite of <u>clean</u> is _____.
7. The opposite of <u>wide</u> is _____.
9. The opposite of <u>difficult</u> is _____.
11. The opposite of <u>loose</u> is _____.
13. The opposite of <u>shallow</u> is _____.

Down:

2. The opposite of <u>push</u> is _____.
4. The opposite of <u>dry</u> is _____.
6. The opposite of <u>asleep</u> is _____.
8. The opposite of <u>up</u> is _____.
10. The opposite of <u>left</u> is _____.
12. The opposite of <u>go</u> is _____.

Match each word with a definition and write it in the correct puzzle box.

Across:

1. little in size
3. finished
5. too
7. prepared
9. fully satisfied
11. another time
13. unusual
15. not ever
17. no noise
19. to stop

Down:

2. one more
4. as a group
6. to remain in one place
8. where one lives
10. boy child to his parents
12. pleased
14. water falling in drops from clouds
16. body in the sky around which the earth moves
18. lovely to look at
20. fast

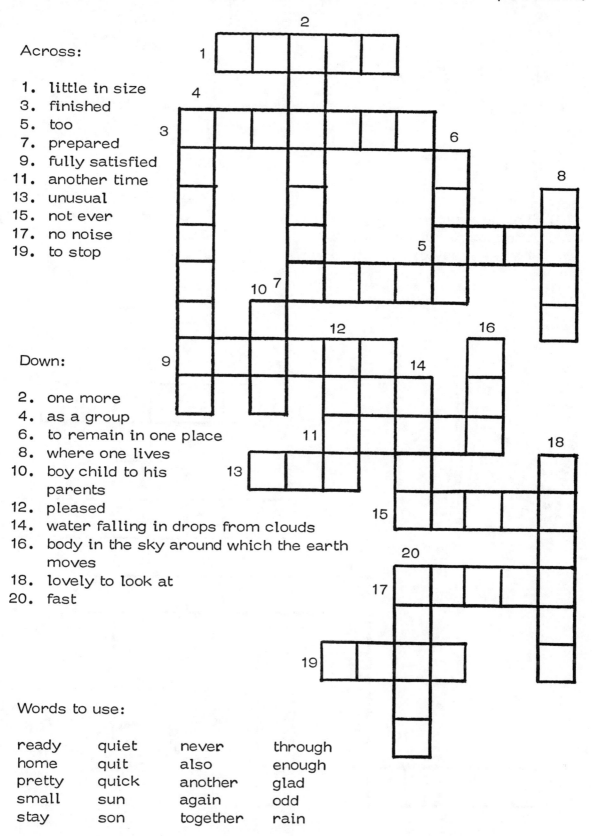

Words to use:

ready	quiet	never	through
home	quit	also	enough
pretty	quick	another	glad
small	sun	again	odd
stay	son	together	rain

SUNDAY
MONDAY
TUESDAY
WEDNESDAY

THURSDAY
FRIDAY
SATURDAY
SUNDAY

DELIGHTFUL DAYS

Match the day of the week to fit the descriptions listed. Write the name of each day in the correct puzzle boxes.

Across:

1. The sixth day of the week
3. The day before Friday
5. The last day of the week
7. The first day of the school week

Down:

2. The day before Thursday
4. The first day of the week
6. The third day of the week

Extra Stuff) Think of other ways to describe each day of the week.

Find these words in the
puzzle and circle them.

CAN   ONE   WE   ON

COME   SEE   THE   TO

NOW   ME   HE

```
O   N   E       S

C   O   M       E

A   T   H       E

N   O   W       E
```

Extra Stuff → Use three of the words that you found
in the puzzle in a sentence.
Illustrate your sentence.

Find and circle all the letters of the alphabet.

Unscramble the money words in the boxes. Draw a line from the word to the matching coin or bill.

lincek
_____

reqruta
_____

ldoarl
_____

idem
_____

ahlf oldlra
_____

npeyn
_____

Extra Stuff → Count the money drawn on this page. What is the total? _____

Answer each problem.
Write the correct number word in the puzzle boxes.

Across	Down
1. $3 + 1 =$	2. $2 \times 1 =$
3. $9 - 2 =$	4. $9 - 4 =$
5. $6 - 5 =$	6. $10 - 7 =$
7. $4 + 6 =$	8. $2 \times 3 =$
9. $2 \times 4 =$	10. $3 + 6 =$

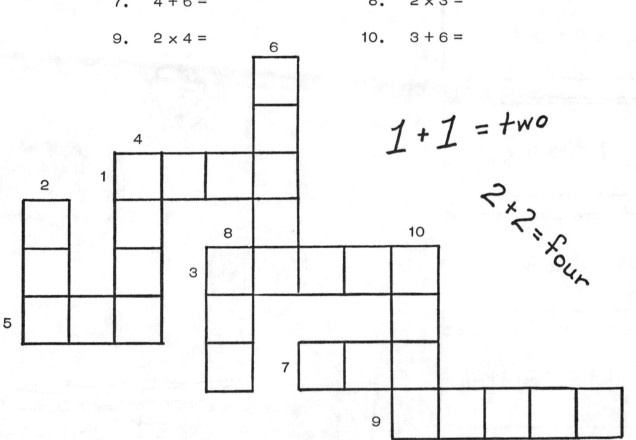

$1 + 1 = two$

$2 + 2 = four$

$2 + 1 = three$

$2 + 3 = five$

Number words to use:

one	six
two	seven
three	eight
four	nine
five	ten

seven 7   eight 8   10 ten

1 one   4 four   9 nine

To solve the puzzle, circle all the number words from 1 to 10.

2

6

n	i	n	e	t
t	e	n	s	h
f	i	v	e	r
o	g	t	v	e
u	h	w	e	e
r	t	o	n	e

5

3

A number word is missing. Which one is it? _____

Extra Stuff → What is the highest number in the puzzle?
What is the lowest number in the puzzle?
Add the highest number to the lowest number. What is their sum?
Subtract the lowest number from the highest number. What is the answer?

275

READY! GET SET! GO!!!!

Find the word to complete each statement and write it in the correct puzzle boxes.

Across:

1. Some people wake up early.
   Others wake up _____ .

3. A lemon tastes sour.
   Sugar tastes _____ .

5. A line going up and down is vertical.
   A line going across is _____ .

7. Summer weather is hot.
   Winter is _____ .

9. A giant is big.
   A baby is _____ .

11. A rock is hard.
    A pillow is _____ .

Down:

2. The floor is below.
   The ceiling is _____ .

4. A snail is slow.
   A rabbit is _____ .

6. The ocean is deep.
   A puddle is _____ .

8. Lifting a book is easy.
   Lifting twenty books is _____ .

10. You put curtains on a window.
    You put rugs on the _____ .

12. A brick is heavy.
    A feather is _____ .

Words to use: light   soft   shallow
                floor   above   little
                difficult fast   late
                horizontal cold   sweet

276

Find a word that rhymes with each puzzle word and write it in the correct puzzle box. (If you need help, the rhyming words to use are listed at the bottom of the page.)

Across:
Rhymes with –

1. sad

3. sat

5. goat

7. pin

9. pill

11. sing

13. rip

Down:
Rhymes with –

2. pail

4. last

6. tack

8. man

10. yellow

12. pig

14. kid

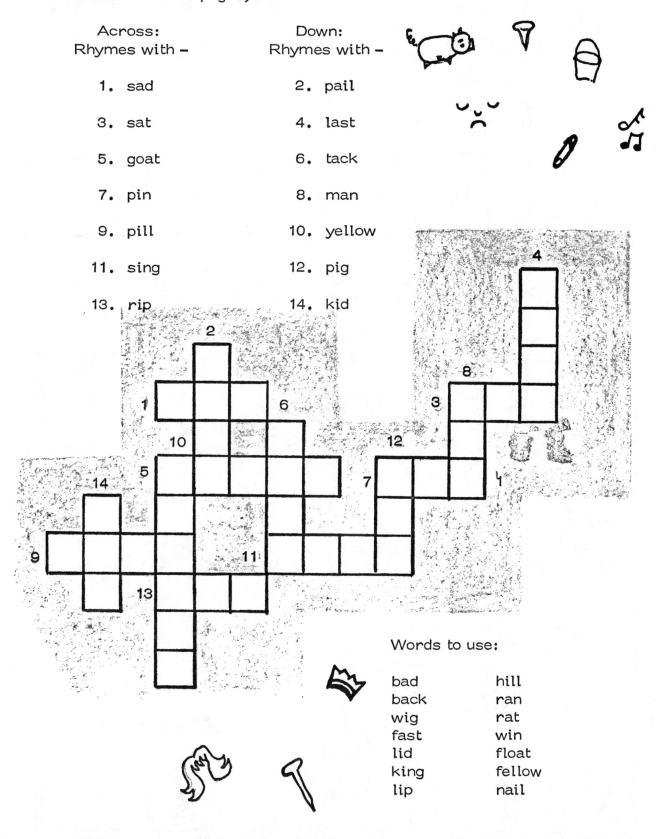

Words to use:

bad	hill
back	ran
wig	rat
fast	win
lid	float
king	fellow
lip	nail

Unscramble the words in your shopping list so you'll know what to buy.

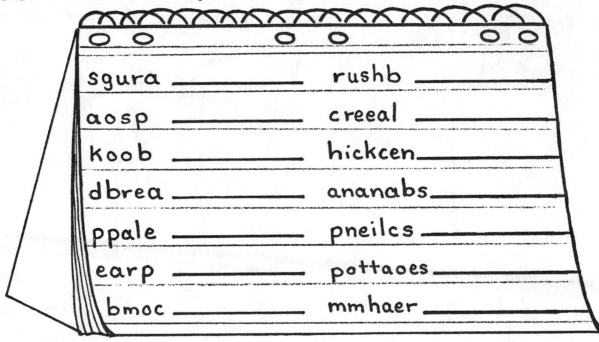

sgura _____	rushb _____
aosp _____	creeal _____
koob _____	hickcen _____
dbrea _____	ananabs _____
ppale _____	pneilcs _____
earp _____	pottaoes _____
bmoc _____	mmhaer _____

Circle the items on your list in the picture below.

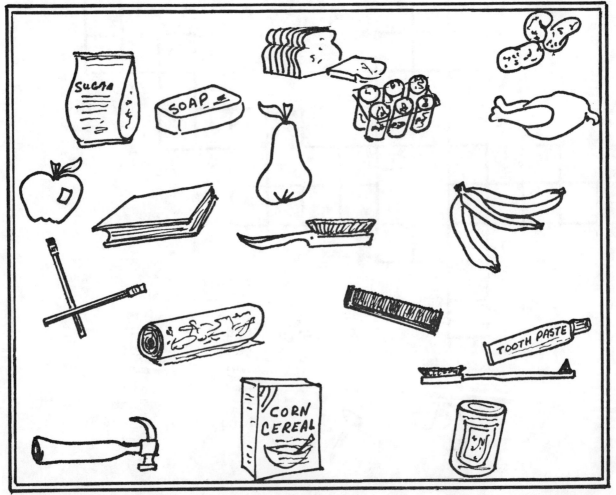

To solve the puzzle, circle all these hidden words.

give
go
going
good
how
once
round
the

Find the letters you have <u>not</u> circled in the puzzle. Unscramble them to make the secret word.

Clue: The pronoun for <u>boy</u> is <u>he</u>.
The pronoun for <u>girl</u> is _____.

Answer: ___ ___ ___

Extra Stuff → Use the words in the puzzle to fill in the blanks:

1. _____ upon a time, there was a giant.

2. _____ do you do?

3. A circle is _____.

4. Where are you _____ after school?

5. The opposite of stop is _____.

Use these words to fill in the sentence formulas on this page:

Nouns	Verbs	Adjectives	Adverbs	Prepositions
children	run	pretty	quickly	on
sidewalk	walk	friendly	loudly	over
trees	talk	handsome	quietly	under
songs	sing	blue		
birds	fly			

Auxiliary Words

the
an
a

Sentence Formula #1:

_____ _____ .
(noun) (verb)

Sentence Formula #2:

_____ _____ _____ .
(adjective) (noun) (verb)

Sentence Formula #3:

_____ _____ _____ .
(noun) (verb) (adverb)

Sentence Formula #4:

_____ _____ _____ .
(noun) (verb) (noun)

Sentence Formula #5:

_____ _____ _____ _____ .
(adjective) (noun) (verb) (adverb)

Sentence Formula #6:

_____ _____ _____ _____ .
(noun) (verb) (preposition) (noun)

Sentence Formula #7:

_____ _____ _____ _____ _____ _____ .
(auxiliary) (noun) (verb) (preposition) (auxiliary) (noun)

SHAPE IN

Name each shape and write the shape words in the correct puzzle boxes.

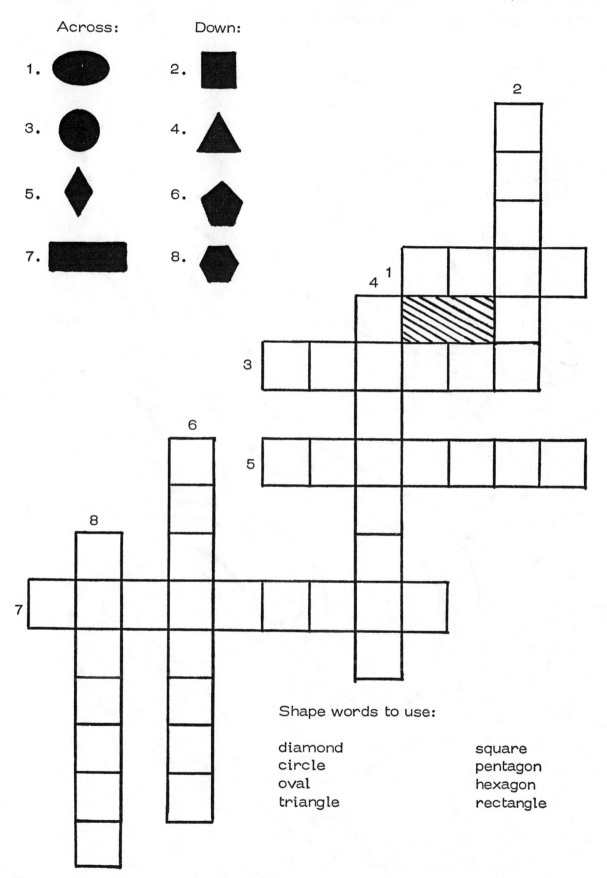

Across:

1.
3.
5.
7.

Down:

2.
4.
6.
8.

Shape words to use:

diamond   square
circle   pentagon
oval   hexagon
triangle   rectangle

WORDY PATH

Find the shortest path from ➜ to ▮ .

Write the words in the path to make a sentence using this formula:

_____ _____ _____ .
    (noun)   (verb)   (adverb)

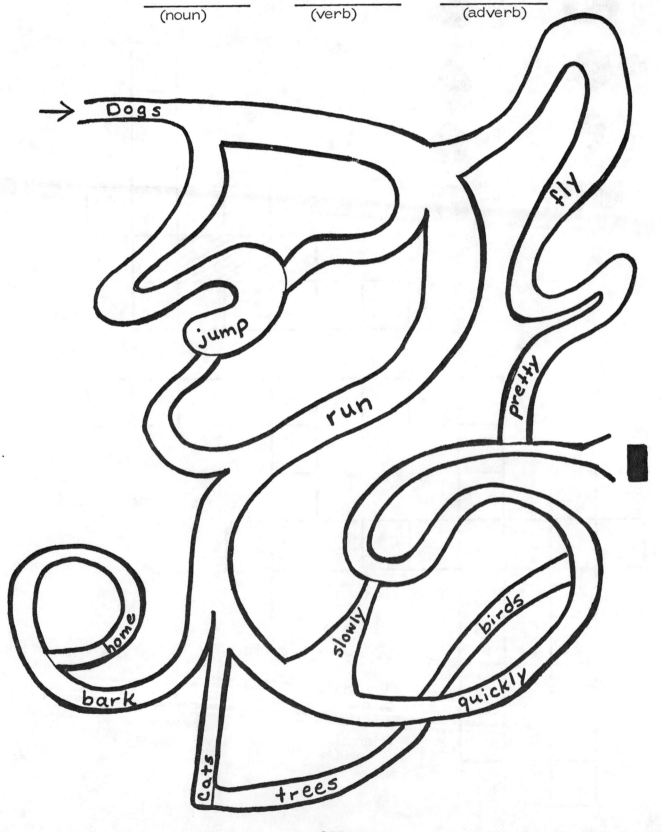

282

WORD RING-AROUND

Find these words in the puzzle and circle them:

all	best	fall	red
an	bet	go	she
as	better	goes	sold
at	call	he	stop
be	cause	keep	to
because	do	old	top
before	dot	read	use

```
a  n  b  e  t  t  e  r
s  b  e  c  a  u  s  e
h  e  f  a  l  l  k  a
e  s  o  l  d  r  e  d
a  t  r  l  o  l  e  t
g  o  e  s  t  o  p  o
```

Extra Stuff ⟶ See how many words you can make using letters in the word BECAUSE.

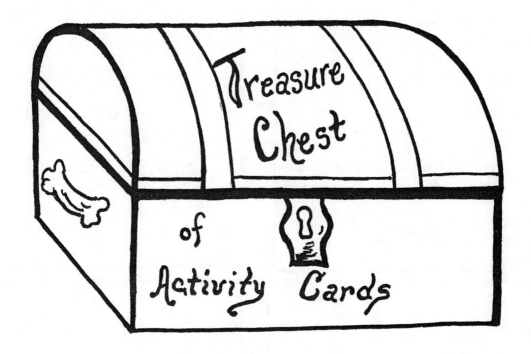

Resourceful teachers know that the first giant step toward maintaining a happy classroom environment is the development of an ample resource file of activities designed to keep students constructively occupied. Creative activities in keeping with the student's current interests are not to be confused with "busy work" such as workbook pages, repetitious math or spelling drills, or other meaningless assignments with little real educational challenge.

The following twelve pages may be pasted on poster board and cut apart to make seventy-two free time activity cards. Each of these activity cards has been designed to stand on its own merit with clearly stated instructions. The activities require only easily assembled materials, culminate in ego reinforcement, and provide motivation for continued use of the activities. Some activity card instructions mandate a quiet setting for individual concentration while others suggest working with one or more friends. The suggested activities are also reflective of various levels of academic difficulty and intellectual involvement. For maximum motivation and full utilization of the card's potential, students should be encouraged to exercise free choice to the fullest and to search out activity cards of real interest to them at the time.

A wooden or metal index card file box or an appropriately sized cardboard box may be painted or covered with metallic gift wrap paper to make an attractive treasure chest to hold the cards. When the "Treasure Chest" is placed in a special classroom spot easily accessible to all students and the ground rules for its use are explained, the fun begins!

Birthday Task:

Write your birth date.

Describe the season in which you were born.

Find your zodiac sign (look in the newspaper and find the Horoscope).

Write a paragraph about a special birthday.

Draw a picture of one special thing you would like to do for your birthday this year.

Draw a picture.

Copy only part of it.

See if a friend can fill in the missing parts.

Compare the two pictures.

Mix the letters in your name and address.

Ask a friend to unscramble them to spell your name.

Look in a book and find:

(1) five words that begin with the letter B (b).

(2) five words that end with the letter D (d).

Draw a map showing the way from the door to your desk.

Look in a dictionary to find the longest word you can.

Write the word.

Ask a friend to find the longest word he can and compare the two.

Be a weatherman.

Give a weather report for the day.

Tell what the weather was like yesterday.

Give a forecast for tomorrow's weather.

Write the names of all of the people in your classroom.

Write the names of ten objects which you can see from your desk.

Write at least ten words that describe winter.

Suggestions: adjectives
                (descriptive words
                like chilly)
                holidays
                clothing
                sports

Use the words in a story. Illustrate your story.

Make your own job description clues and ask a friend to guess who you are.

Suggestions: postman
                milkman
                bus driver
                teacher
                carpenter
                plumber
                electrician
                gardener
                waiter
                beautician
                grocer

Write descriptions of at least ten things that you can do in the summertime.

Write ten descriptions of things that you cannot do in the summertime.

Draw and write a description of an outfit you would like to wear for each season of the year.

Ask a friend to talk with you about fear.

Write a paragraph about the differences in your fears and your friend's fears.

Write an essay about good manners and when and where to use them.

List as many makes of automobiles as you can. Ask a friend to make a list and compare the two lists.

Write sentences using the past tense of these verbs:

fly
sing
swim
give
read

Write an original riddle and ask a friend to guess the answer.

Ask your friend to write a riddle for you to guess.

Write some silly statements and ask a friend to tell you what is wrong with each statement.

Example:

I got up this morning and washed my bed.

Make a glossary of events, new words, names, or terms used in print on the front page of your local newspaper.

Begin a story with:

"Once upon a time there was a funny goat who..."

Ask friends to add a sentence to the story until the story is finished.

Illustrate your story.

Make an announcement to your classmates.

Use one of the following topics:

(1) cookie sale
(2) class party
(3) homework assignment

Act out different action words and ask a friend to guess what you are doing.

Examples: run   crawl
           walk   laugh
           hop   talk
           jump   eat

Pretend you are a disc jockey on a local radio station.

Select a few records to be played and write what you will say before you play them.

Put small words together to make longer words that are the names of foods.

Examples: popcorn
           pineapple

Write a story using ten of the words you made.

Use the names of your classmates to make a crossword puzzle.

Make a list of all the tools that can be found in a classroom.

Make a list of all the animals that you can think of.

How many of these animals can be found on a farm? in the jungle? in a home? in the zoo?

Write the names of six eating tools.

Write the names of six writing tools.

Write the names of six carpenter's tools.

Write the names of some other tools and tell what they are used for.

List as many things as you can that might be found in a lady's purse.

Write all the words you can think of that end with the word "day".

Examples: Sunday
             birthday

Write a journal for a week.

For each day list all of the things that you do and the ways that you feel.

Make a list of twenty words that start with the letter "s". (Example: snake, swallow, silly)

Make a story using these words.

List words that belong to each category below:

    colors
    toys
    family members
    countries
    bodies of water

Circle the word that does not belong in each group of words below.

Monday   radio   car
Tuesday   television   truck
Wednesday   train   taxi
February   book   road

        paper   apple
        pencil   spinach
        pen   banana
        crayon   peach

Use this code –

1	2	3	4	5	6	7	8	9	0
R	D	I	H	B	C	F	N	E	A

to find the names coded in the telephone numbers below:

        136-4012
        501-5010
        719-2239
        591-8369
        195-9660

Follow a person in the news (such as a governor, movie star, astronaut). Collect newspaper articles and clippings on the person and make a report on his or her activities.

Find a word in the dictionary.
Write only the definition of the
word and ask a friend to guess
the word.

Draw a picture of an event
that could make someone cry.

Draw a picture of an event that
could make someone laugh.

Make new words by adding
silent "e" to these words:

mad	shin
fin	rip
hid	bar
bit	dim
hat	star
scrap	not

Use the words in sentences.

Make these adjectives into
nouns by adding the
suffix "ness":

good
sweet
high

Use the words in sentences.

Write a poem using words that
rhyme with "rat".

Illustrate your poem.

Find a cartoon series in the
newspaper. Cut out the words
in the blurbs.

Write in your own ideas to make
a new story.

Use your spelling words to make your own word search puzzle.

Make a floor plan of your classroom.

Locate each person's desk and write his or her name on the desk.

Find the first animal listed in the dictionary.

Find the last animal listed in the dictionary.

Make a schedule for your day tomorrow.

Start with the time you plan to get out of bed. List other things you want to do and arrange for the time to do them.

Draw a picture of yourself.

Draw a picture of yourself as a baby.

Draw a picture of yourself as you think you will look next year.

Make a list of compound words using color words. (Example: rosebud)

Illustrate your words.

Color words to use:

red	pink	white
blue	yellow	rose
black	green	tan

(Use your dictionary for extra help!)

Write as many words as you can think of that rhyme with:

hat	big
can	pot
deep	back
dog	care
tear	jolly
sad	pick

Race with a friend to see who can write the most words.

(a)   Draw a picture of your house.

(b)   Draw a picture of your room.

(c)   Take your pictures home to share with your family.

Look in a mirror.   Draw a picture of yourself.

Now, draw a picture of how you think you will look twenty years from now.

Look in a textbook and find:

(a) three words that have two e's.

(b) three words that have two o's.

(c) three words that have two l's.

Write the words.

Use the dictionary to find ten words which, spelled backward, make the same word.

Example: mom – mom

Use the dictionary to find ten words which, spelled backward, make a different word.

Example: pat – tap

Write the words.

Look in the dictionary to find at least three definitions for each of these words:

      scale
      trunk
      band

Discuss the definitions with a friend.

Add a letter to each word to make a new word. Hints are given for each word.

    boa (to sail in)
    plane (moves around the sun)
    room (to sweep with)
    late (to eat from)
    bake (one who bakes)

Illustrate the new words.

Draw a picture of the animal that makes each of the following sounds:

      neigh
      bray
      squeak
      bark
      meow
      yelp
      chirp

Make a menu for a fancy restaurant you would like to own.

Design a cover for the menu.

Draw a picture of the outside of the restaurant and arrange a window display to attract customers.

List at least three things you like about school.

List at least three things you dislike about school.

Write a story about a "perfect school day" which includes all the things you like and none of the things you dislike.

Write a script for a television special honoring the principal of your school. Be sure to include events about the principal's past and present life and his hopes for the future of the school.

Write ten words ending with "ed".

Write twenty words ending with "ing".

Write a newspaper story.

Tell what happened in class, at home, or on the way to school.

Find a silly picture in a magazine or book and write a story about it.

Write a description of a friend. Tell how he or she looks, how he or she is dressed, and anything else you can think of to help your classmates guess who the friend is.

Draw three incomplete pictures.

Ask a friend to tell what is missing in each picture.

Write sentences using these prepositions:

to	by
up	around
upon	of
after	over

List all of the things that a boy or girl can do. (Examples: run, walk, hop, jump, work, play)

Do the same thing for a cat, a teacher, a dog, a tiger, and a frog.

How are they alike?

How are they different?

Use a favorite story or book as the plot for a play. Write the play and ask classmates to help present it to the class.

Write a situation story requiring the following types of voices:

    baby with a tiny voice
    woman with a medium voice
    man with a deep voice
    animal with a growl

Write a paragraph describing a game or sport. Ask a friend to guess what the sport is.

Begin a story about one of the following topics:

    The day the teacher stayed home
    The first snowstorm of the season
    The circus clown's birthday party
    The disappearance of the traffic
       sign

Ask a friend to finish the story.

Make a scrapbook of beginning word sounds.

Make one page of words beginning with each of the following sounds:

B	N
D	R
S	T
P	G
M	F

HIGH INTEREST-LOW VOCABULARY BOOKS FOR STUDENTS

Title – Publisher	Reading Grade Level Range	Interest Grade Level Range
All About Books Random House	4 – 6	5 – 11
American Adventure Series Harper and Row	2 – 6	4 – 9
American Heritage Series Aladdin Books, American Book Company	5 – 6	5 – 9
Basic Vocabulary Series Garrard Publications	1 – 3	2 – 4
Beginner Books Random House	1 – 2	1 – 4
Checkered Flag Series Field Educational Publications	2	6 – 11
Cowboy Sam Books Benefic Press	1 – 3	1 – 4
Curriculum Motivation Series Lyons & Carnahan	1 – 4	1 – 6
Dan Frontier Books Benefic Press	1 – 3	1 – 7
Deep Sea Adventure Series Field Educational Publications	2 – 4	3 – 9
Dimensions in Reading Series Science Research Associates	3 – 7	9 – 12
Discovery Books Garrard Publications	2 – 4	3 – 6
Every Reader Library Webster Division, McGraw-Hill	4 – 5	4 – 10
First Books Franklin Watts	3 – 5	3 – 8

HIGH INTEREST–LOW VOCABULARY BOOKS FOR STUDENTS

Title – Publisher	Reading Grade Level Range	Interest Grade Level Range
Folklore of the World Books Garrard Publications	3	2 – 8
Gateway Books Random House	2 – 3	3 – 9
Getting to Know Books E. M. Hale	4 – 5	5 – 9
Jim Forest Readers Field Educational Publications	1 – 3	3 – 6
Landmark Books Random House	5 – 7	5 – 11
Middle–Grade Book Series Children's Press	4	3 – 7
Modern Adventure Series Harper and Row	4 – 6	4 – 11
Morgan Bay Series Field Educational Publications	2 – 4	4 – 9
Pleasure Reading Series Garrard Publications	3 – 4	3 – 5
Reader's Digest Skill Builders Reader's Digest Services	2 – 6	2 – 9
Reading Attainment System Grolier Educational Corp.	3 – 6	6 – 12
Sailor Jack Books Benefic Press	1 – 3	2 – 7
Signal Books Doubleday and Company	4	5 – 9
Space Age Books Benefic Press	2 – 3	2 – 6

HIGH INTEREST–LOW VOCABULARY BOOKS FOR STUDENTS

Title – Publisher	Reading Grade Level Range	Interest Grade Level Range
Step-Up Books Random House	2 – 3	3 – 9
Strange Teen-Age Tales Books D. C. Heath	5 – 6	5 – 11
Teen-Age Tales D. C. Heath	4 – 6	6 – 11
True Books Children's Press	2 – 3	1 – 6
We Were There Books E. M. Hale	4 – 5	5 – 9
Wildlife Adventure Series Field Educational Publications	2 – 4	3 – 8
World Landmark Books Random House	5 – 6	5 – 11

ADDITIONAL REFERENCES

HIGH INTEREST-LOW VOCABULARY BOOKS FOR STUDENTS

ADDITIONAL REFERENCES

Title – Publisher	Reading Grade Level Range	Interest Grade Level Range

SELECTED TEACHER REFERENCES

EXCEPTIONALITY

Blanco, R. Prescriptions for Children with Learning and Adjustment Problems. Springfield: Charles C. Thomas, Publishers, 1972.

Dunn, L. Exceptional Children in the Schools. 2nd ed. New York: Holt, Rinehart and Winston, Inc., 1973.

Ekwall, E. Locating and Correcting Reading Difficulties. Columbus, Ohio: Charles E. Merrill Publishing Co., 1970.

Gearhart, B. Learning Disabilities: Educational Strategies. St. Louis: Webster Division, McGraw-Hill Book Company, 1968.

Hewett, F. Education of Exceptional Learners. Boston: Allyn and Bacon, Inc., 1975.

Kephart, N. The Slow Learner in the Classroom. rev. ed. Columbus, Ohio: Charles E. Merrill Publishing Co., 1971.

Kirk, S. Educating Exceptional Children. 2nd ed. Boston: Houghton Mifflin Co., 1972.

Lerner, J. Children with Learning Disabilities. Boston: Houghton Mifflin Co., 1971.

Mann, P. and P. Suiter. Handbook in Diagnostic Teaching. Boston: Allyn and Bacon, Inc., 1974.

Murdock, J. The Other Children: An Introduction to Exceptionality. New York: Harper and Row, Publishers, 1975.

Sanderlin, O. Teaching Gifted Children. New York: A. S. Barnes and Co., 1973.

Wallace, G. and J. McLoughlin. Learning Disabilities: Concepts and Characteristics. Columbus, Ohio: Charles E. Merrill Publishing Co., 1975.

HUMANISTIC AND CREATIVE CLASSROOM ORGANIZATION

Berman, L. M. New Priorities in the Curriculum. Columbus, Ohio: Charles E. Merrill Publishing Co., 1968.

Britton, L. Creative and Mental Growth. Englewood Cliffs, New Jersey: Prentice-Hall, Inc., 1971.

Buscaglia, Leo. <u>Love</u>. Thorofare, New Jersey: Charles B. Slack, Inc., 1972.

Carswell, E. M. and D. Roubinek. <u>Open Sesame</u>. Pacific Palesades, California: Goodyear Publishing Co., 1974.

Casteel, D. and R. Stahl. <u>Value Clarification in the Classroom: A Primer</u>. Pacific Palisades, California: Goodyear Publishing Co., 1975.

Chase, L. <u>The Other Side of the Report Card</u>. Pacific Palisades, California: Goodyear Publishing Co., 1975.

Forte, I. and J. MacKenzie. <u>Nooks, Crannies and Corners, Learning Centers for Creative Classrooms</u>. Nashville, Tenn.: Incentive Publications, Inc., 1973.

Goodlad, J. I., M. F. Klein and Associates. <u>Behind the Classroom Door</u>. Worthington, Ohio: Charles A. Jones Publishing Company, 1970.

Gowan, J. C. <u>Development of the Creative Individual</u>. San Diego: Robert R. Knapp, Publisher, 1972.

Greer, M. and B. Rubinstein. <u>Will the Real Teacher Please Stand Up?</u> Pacific Palisades, California: Goodyear Publishing Co., 1972.

Johnson, K. R. <u>Teaching the Culturally Disadvantaged</u>. Palo Alto, California: Science Research Associates, Inc., 1970.

Manning, D. <u>Toward A Humanistic Curriculum</u>. New York: Harper and Row, Publishers, 1971.

Purkey, W. W. <u>Self Concept and School Achievement</u>. Englewood Cliffs, New Jersey: Prentice-Hall, Inc., 1970.

Raths, L. E. <u>Meeting the Needs of Children</u>. Columbus, Ohio: Charles E. Merrill Publishing Co., 1972.

Romey, W. D. <u>Risk-Trust-Love: Learning in a Humane Environment</u>. Columbus, Ohio: Charles E. Merrill Publishing Co., 1972.

Stephens, L. S. <u>Teachers' Guide to Open Education</u>. New York: Holt, Rinehart and Winston, Inc., 1974.

Torrance, E. P. <u>Encouraging Creativity in the Classroom</u>. Dubuque, Iowa: William C. Brown Co., 1970.

Torrance, E. P. and R. E. Meyers. <u>Creative Learning and Teaching</u>. New York: Dodd, Mead Inc., 1970.

LANGUAGE ARTS

Burns, P. C. and B. L. Broman. The Language Arts in Childhood Education. 3rd ed. Chicago: Rand McNally College Publishing Co., 1975.

Burrows, A. T., D. L. Monson and R. G. Stauffer. New Horizons in the Language Arts. New York: Harper and Row, Publishers, 1972.

Corcoran, G. B. Language Arts in the Elementary School: A Modern Linguistic Approach. New York: The Ronald Press Company, 1970.

Dallmann, M. Teaching the Language Arts in the Elementary School. Dubuque, Iowa: William C. Brown Co., 1971.

Forte, I., M. Pangle and R. Tupa. Cornering Creative Writing. Nashville, Tenn.: Incentive Publications, Inc., 1974.

Forte, I. and J. MacKenzie. Kids' Stuff, Reading and Language Experiences, Primary. 2nd ed. Nashville, Tenn.: Incentive Publications, Inc., 1974.

Forte, I., J. MacKenzie and M. Frank. Kids' Stuff, Reading and Language Experiences, Intermediate-Jr. High. Nashville, Tenn.: Incentive Publications, Inc., 1973.

Funk, H. and D. Triplett. Language Arts in the Elementary School. Philadelphia: J. B. Lippincott Company, 1972.

Greene, H. A. and W. T. Petty. Developing Language Skills in the Elementary Schools. 4th ed. Boston: Allyn and Bacon, Inc., 1971.

Lamb, P. Guiding Children's Language Learning. 2nd ed. Dubuque, Iowa: William C. Brown Co., 1971.

Logan, L. M., V. G. Logan and L. Peterson. Creative Communication: Teaching the Language Arts. Toronto: McGraw-Hill Ryerson Limited, 1972.

McCaslin, N. Children and Drama. New York: David McKay Company, Inc., 1975.

Petty, W., D. Petty and M. Becking. Experiences in Language: Tools and Techniques for Language Arts Methods. Boston: Allyn and Bacon, Inc., 1973.

Rubin, D. Teaching Elementary Language Arts. New York: Holt, Rinehart and Winston, Inc., 1975.

Smith, J. A. Adventures in Communication. Boston: Allyn and Bacon, Inc., 1972.

Smith, J. A. Creative Teaching of the Language Arts in the Elementary School. 2nd ed. Boston: Allyn and Bacon, Inc., 1973.

READING

Bush, C. L. and M. H. Huebner. Strategies for Reading in the Elementary School. New York: The Macmillan Company, 1970.

Cohen, S. A. Teach Them All to Read. New York: Random House, 1969.

Dallman, M., R. L. Rouch, L. Y. C. Chang and J. J. DeBoer. The Teaching of Reading. 4th ed. New York: Holt, Rinehart and Winston, Inc., 1974.

Durkin, D. Teaching Them to Read. 2nd ed. Boston: Allyn and Bacon, Inc., 1974.

Farnette, C., I. Forte and B. Loss. Kids' Stuff, Reading and Writing Readiness. Nashville, Tenn.: Incentive Publications, Inc., 1975.

Fry, E. B. Reading Instruction for Classroom and Clinic. New York: McGraw-Hill Book Company, 1972.

Harris, A. J. and E. R. Sipay. How to Increase Reading Ability. 6th ed. New York: David McKay Company, Inc., 1975.

Harris, L. and C. B. Smith. Reading Instruction Through Diagnostic Teaching. New York: Holt, Rinehart and Winston, Inc., 1972.

Heilman, A. W. Principles and Practices of Teaching Reading. 3rd ed. Columbus, Ohio: Charles E. Merrill Publishing Co., 1972.

Karlin, R. Perspectives on Elementary Reading – Principles and Strategies of Teaching. New York: Harcourt, Brace and Jovanovich, Inc., 1973.

Lowerre, G. and A. Scandura. Critical Reading: Learning Programs Engineered to Behavioral Specifications. Worthington, Ohio: Charles A. Jones Publishing Company, 1973.

Miller, L. L. Developing Reading Efficiency. 3rd ed. Minneapolis, Minn.: Burgess Publishing Co., 1972.

Shepherd, D. Comprehensive High School Reading Methods. Columbus, Ohio: Charles E. Merrill Publishing Co., 1973.

Smith, J. A. Creative Teaching of Reading in the Elementary School. Boston: Allyn and Bacon, Inc., 1975.

Smith, R. J. and T. C. Barrett. Teaching Reading in the Middle Grades. Reading, Mass.: Addison-Wesley Publishing Company, 1974.

Spache, G. D. Good Reading for Poor Readers. Champaign, Illinois: Garrard Publishing Company, 1974.

Spache, G. D. Good Reading for the Disadvantaged Reader. Champaign, Illinois: Garrard Publishing Company, 1975.

Veatch, J., and Others. Key Words to Reading. The Language Experience Approach Begins. Columbus, Ohio: Charles E. Merrill Publishing Co., 1973.

Wallen, C. J. Competency in Teaching Reading. Chicago: Science Research Associates, Inc., 1972.

Zintz, M. V. The Reading Process. Dubuque, Iowa: William C. Brown Company, 1975.

Notes

Notes

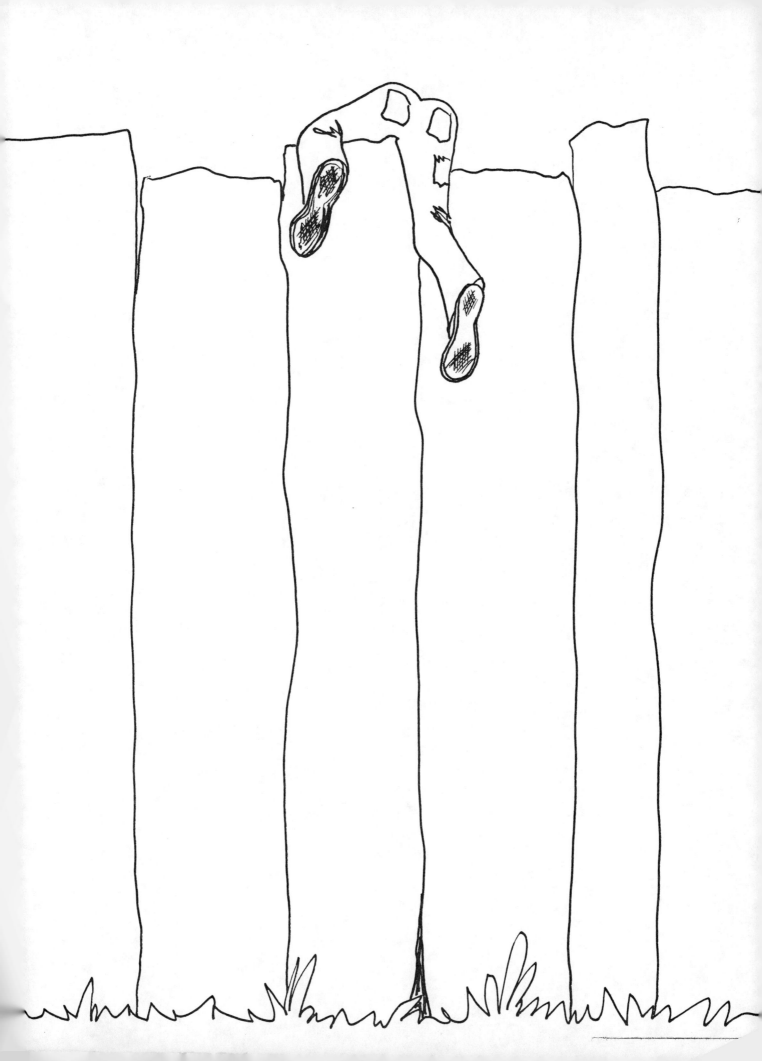